"Ten Spiritual Truths for Successful Living for Gays and Lesbians"*

(...and everyone else!)*

Discovering Positive Spirituality for Gays and Lesbians on the Journey of Faith

The Rev. Troy D. Perry, Author

Library of Congress Control Number: 2003093983
ISBN: 0-9741793-0-2

Printed in the United States by
Morris Publishing
3212 East Highway 30
Kearney, NE 68847
1-800-650-7888

This book is dedicated to the love of my life, Phillip Ray De Blieck,
one of the kindest men I have ever met.

His life is filled with love for all of God's creation –
love for flowers and animals and people.

I admire his deep spirituality and am thankful that he has chosen
to love me unconditionally.

It is always so hard when I sit down to write an acknowledgment page. I just don't want to forget anyone.

First, I want to thank Jim Birkitt for acting as my editor on this book. After I produced the original manuscript, Jim was invaluable in helping me to rewrite and fine tune this book.

I want to thank William (Bill) Tom for taking the photograph that is on the cover. It is a photograph of my partner, Phillip, and me as I spoke before 800,000 people at the Millennium March on Washington for Equality in April of 2000.

I wish to thank, as always, my long-time Confidential Assistant, Frank Zerilli, who acted as the chief proofreader for this book. I also want to thank two friends, Don Pence and Mark Hahn who gave of their time to read my original manuscript and lovingly made suggestions to improve the text.

I want to thank Roman Cardenas for the work he did as graphic artist on the book and for his assistance with proofreading the book.

I also want to thank my partner, Phillip Ray De Blieck for helping me type the original manuscript.

To all of you who are part of this book through your stories – thank you. And last but not least, I want to thank the membership of the Metropolitan Community Churches who have given me their love and patience for these last 35 years of ministry as the Founder, Moderator and Pastor of the MCC Movement.

If I have forgotten anyone who helped me with the book even though I didn't mention your name, please accept this as my thank you.

As I write these words, I am busily looking forward to and preparing for the 35th anniversary celebration of Metropolitan Community Churches, the world's largest and oldest church group with a primary, affirming ministry to gays, lesbians, bisexuals, and transgender persons.

By their very nature, anniversaries are times to reflect and look back. This anniversary has given me time to pause in my own personal journey of faith and to review my life and work.

And one thing is sure: It's been an exciting journey and a constant adventure these past 35 years.

On October 6, 1968 (one year before the Stonewall Riots), 12 people gathered in my home in Huntington Beach in the Los Angeles area for a worship service. But as time would prove, this was no ordinary church service.

This story is told in more detail in my earlier books, but here's a quick summary. I was a minister who was ex-communicated from my church for being gay. Following a suicide attempt, I began to again sense God's presence in my life. It was then that hope returned. My spiritual faith grew stronger. And along the way I discovered the keys to reconcile my sexuality with my spirituality.

Out of these experiences, an idea was born – an idea that there could be a spiritual center for gay, lesbian, bisexual and transgender persons where we could discover God, develop our spirituality and deepen our faith.

The idea became a dream... the dream became my passion... and the passion became my life's work.

And in the midst of my work and ministry, wonderful,

unbelievable, miraculous experiences have come to pass.

During these past 35 years, MCC has grown from those first 12 persons who worshiped in my living room to more than 46,000 gays, lesbians, bisexuals, transgender persons and enlightened heterosexuals – and continues to grow week by week. MCC groups can now be found in 23 countries of the world and people in 25 other countries have written for assistance in beginning an MCC congregation.

Out of these past 35 years, I have discovered ten spiritual truths – principles – for successful living as open, proud gay, lesbian, bisexual and transgender persons – ten truths that can powerfully change negative attitudes into positive ones... that can turn desperate situations into hope-filled ones... that can bring focus and purpose into lives that are drifting and unfulfilled.

(If you are heterosexual, keep reading. These spiritual truths are universal truths, with application to all people.)

Over three decades, I have spoken to, counseled, helped and ministered to tens of thousands of persons. Everything within my being tells me that the study and practice of these ten principles can make any life – yes, your life! – richer, fuller and more meaningful.

Before we go any further, let's talk heart to heart. I want you to know where I'm coming from.

While there are powerful truths to be learned from every spiritual path (it may surprise you how many truths show up in many religious communities), I have discovered my greatest fulfillment through the study of the Hebrew and Christian Scriptures, which we call the Bible.

Now, that makes some of my friends a bit defensive. And believe me, I understand if that is your initial reaction!

Please hear me out.

The very first step in reconciling our sexuality and spirituality is to realize that God and God's followers aren't necessarily on the same wave length. That's part of the "human dilemma." Many religions have allowed human-based traditions to creep into beliefs. Others have adopted society's standards rather than God's standards. And some religious leaders have exercised their own control issues and internal emotional problems – and then imposed them on their religious followers!

You get the picture.

This is part of the work that I – along with the leadership, ministers and members of MCC – have been called to do. During the past 35 years, we have attempted to remove the cultural biases and negative societal factors that have been imposed on Christianity.

And in this process, we've achieved two historic accomplishments:

First, we have liberated the Bible and reclaimed the Scriptures as a positive document for people from every walk of life. The Bible can no longer be held captive by individual religious denominations, religious leaders, or televangelists. The Bible is not a tool to control people, nor to hurt people, nor to limit people. When truly understood in its historical context, the Bible is filled with messages of positive faith, hope and affirmation for all people. And that most certainly includes lesbians, gays, bisexuals and transgender persons.

Second, we have worked to reclaim the Infinite God who is revealed through Jesus Christ as Unconditional Love. If you're still reading with me, I want to tell you that this one thought – the teaching that God is revealed as Unconditional Love – is, for many people, the single most powerful, liberating, life-changing thought they will ever think. It changes how we view our lives... our worth... our relationship to the universe and to God.

Here is one final thought to set the stage for our journey of exploration into the "Ten Spiritual Truths." Please listen to me carefully:

I cannot tell you how many times I've been asked, "Rev. Perry, how do you know you're not just using the Holy Scriptures to justify your own homosexuality?"

Now, that's a really good question! Please, please listen to my heart. There are two powerful answers to this important question.

The first is that throughout my life, I have had a genuine desire to discover God's plan for us. I have genuinely wanted to know God's heart and understand God's will. I have never been content with excuses or justifications. And – to be perfectly blunt – I have no desire to deceive myself. That would really be a short-sighted course of action. No, my desire has always been for truth!

I guess that's why the question that has always been difficult for me to understand. In my ministry with tens of thousands of people, I have never met one person who wanted easy answers from me at the expense of the truth. My honest search for God's plan for gays, lesbians, bisexuals and transgender persons has forged my ministry and is embodied in this book.

Second – and now I ask you to really hear my heart – I have lived long enough to say, humbly but truthfully, that I have lived and ministered these past 35 years as the founder and moderator of MCC with integrity and honesty.

With whatever challenges I have confronted in life, I have attempted to live and minister with integrity and honesty. And I have brought these same characteristics to MCC's ground-breaking work of integrating spirituality and sexuality. I have staked my own personal integrity upon this work.

And that sets the stage to begin our journey of exploration together.

It is my prayer that along this journey, each of us will discover – and rediscover! – God's positive, hope-filled message for our lives. Come join me on the journey!

CHAPTER ONE
God Did Not Create You So God Could Have Someone To Hate

I wish I could sit down with you – just the two of us – and talk with you. I wish we could talk and share together until the theme of this chapter sinks deep into your subconscious and becomes part of your person... part of your thought process... part of your life.

Yes, if we could sit down together, just the two of us, one-on-one, and if I could only convey one message to you, this would be it:

"God did not create you so God could have someone to hate."

To grasp – really grasp – this principle is to find incredible liberation in your life!

In my lifetime, I have talked and corresponded with thousands of gay, lesbian, bisexual and transgender persons who believed God hated them because of their sexuality.

Why do people still believe this?

–Negative, reactionary religions have spread that message.

–Televangelists have used it to spread fear and raise funds.

–Too many churches have repeated the negative spiritual messages they were taught, instead of what God teaches.

–Politicians have used it to get votes.

–Governments have continued to reinforce this negative message through inaction and failure to protect the rights of all citizens.

Whew! No wonder so many people have believed this negative message. Sometimes it seems like this negativity pummels us from all directions: religion, culture, organizations, society and politicians.

In their negativity, they have twisted God's message of love and acceptance into rejection and judgment. And they do it through words.

As any human being knows, words can hurt! Everyone of us can remember times when words were used to hurt us. Many of us immediately think back to childhood – to words that had the power to frighten us, upset us, and make us feel inferior.

Human beings use words in subtle (and not so subtle) ways to convey our feelings about other humans. The use of language in this way is as old as our existence on earth. We use language to evoke emotion. We want – indeed, we need – people to respond to us. To be ignored is paramount to not existing.

There are three important lessons here.

First, we want to be noticed. It's important to our psyche that others are aware that we are a part of the human family, not that we are just human. Newborn babies are one of the best examples of this truth.

Observation of newborns has taught us that babies who

are communicated with (i.e.; talked to, held, given love to) live; those who don't receive these forms of caring and communication die.

A friend of mine, who is a maternity nurse, shared with me that during the start of the HIV/AIDS pandemic, before anyone understood what caused AIDS, many hospitals discouraged their staff from touching babies who were born HIV positive. These babies had minimal contact with other humans.

They were fed, their diapers were changed – and they died very quickly. It was only after hospital staff overcame the fear of HIV and started treating these babies like any others in their charge that these children started living for years instead of days.

As children we love to be noticed – noticed by our parents, our extended family, and even strangers. It's part of our human condition to need and want acceptance!

There is a second lesson that we human beings have learned. We are taught by whatever culture we are raised in, that the giving and receiving of love is the most vital need of human beings. For humans not to share in this emotion is to be considered an outcast.

In past centuries, to be an outcast meant that the larger culture had relegated you to the status of a non-person. The culture dictated how you were to be treated by everyone around you. You might be loved, or you might not be loved. Human beings have used language to enforce the will of the larger culture on persons it viewed to be outcasts. As a long-time member of the Christian clergy, I can testify that I have witnessed this in the so-called Christian culture.

In my own lifetime I have seen human beings use negative words in order to deprive others of their personhood. I have learned that if we can turn a person into a label – instead of seeing them as a fellow human – we can quickly justify any action we wish to take against that person, even withholding the emotion all humans need: love.

Whatever culture we have been raised in, we have been taught to seek both love and acceptance from our peers. It's just the way it is.

There is a third lesson (not a truth, mind you, a lesson) that our cultures teach us.

Our larger culture expects us to conform to its standards in the areas of family, law, and religion. In many parts of the world, conformity is regrettably viewed as more important to the welfare of a culture than love or acceptance. Again, subtle and not so subtle messages are communicated to humans all their lives about their need (whether it's true or not) to conform to their culture.

As a Christian clergyperson who also happens to be a gay man, and who has witnessed his own culture in the USA respond to demands from the lesbian and gay community for change in the way the larger culture views them, I can share my own observations of how I believe you can know without hesitation that God did not create you so God could have someone to hate!

I know I am a product of the American culture in which I was raised. I was born into a loving family. I am the oldest of five sons. I was taught to love family, religion, and country. I loved my family and was loved unconditionally by them. My parents introduced me to the Christian faith and I fell "head over heels" in love with it.

I knew that church was where I belonged from the moment I first walked thought the door. I know I received my call to ministry when I was thirteen years old. I was licensed to preach in the Baptist faith at age fifteen. At age eighteen I married. By age nineteen I was pastoring my first church. By the time I was twenty-three, my wife and I were the proud parents of two sons. At age twenty five I was drafted into the US Army as my county was at war. I went willing to serve my country as my culture had taught me to. I know I would have willingly died to protect my country had that been required of me. I willingly conformed to my culture. After all, it was for family, God, and country!

This is the truth just as I experienced it, but the truth is never simple.

My view of American culture and my early conformity to it is not the same for other Americans. For African Americans and other minorities, racism was the order of the day in the America in which I was born. Slavery as an institution had only been outlawed eighty-five years before my birth.

Segregation was a way on life in most of the USA when I was growing up. I vividly remember hearing the awful stories of the lynching that had taken place during my lifetime not far from the town in which I was raised. These were difficult, painful times in American history for our African American sisters and brothers.

Conformity to the culture meant they accepted the fact that the US Constitution was not widely interpreted as applicable to them by the dominant white culture. In fact, a majority of the white population used many terrible means to infer that African Americans were inferior to the larger community.

I grew up in a church that helped keep that status quo in place. As much as I loved the churches I grew up in, they were, and too often still are, the most racist institutions in America. Their use of sacred scriptures – selectively and out of context – as a tool to subjugate minorities in America should still be a cause of shame for all religious communities in the United States.

It has been said, and it is true, that Sunday morning worship hour is the most segregated hour in America.

In fact, large numbers of churches in America were affected by the Civil War. Entire religious denominations were torn apart by the actions of theologians who debated the interpretation of scripture as it related to the institution of slavery. Many denominations sided with slave owners, believing preachers who taught that African Americans were inferior and that the scriptures approved of slavery.

(Do you remember my introduction? Remember my advice not to judge God by God's followers? The fact that people have misrepresented God and twisted God's truth is in no way a negative reflection on God. It's a negative reflection on the human ability to impose our own cultural biases and personal prejudices on others. One of my favorite bumper stickers is a simple prayer that reads, "Jesus, deliver us from your followers." That's a prayer to which I can always say a hearty "Amen!")

But back to the point. Many religious leaders in the USA during the time of the Civil War told stories to their slaves from the Hebrew Scriptures – stories that proposed to teach them that "Father Abraham," who God called to be the first Patriarch of the children of Israel, owned slaves and that nowhere in the Hebrew Scriptures did God condemn slavery. In fact African slaves were told their skin color was the result of a curse – a curse they claimed was placed on them by God when Ham (a son of Noah) looked at his father's nakedness [Genesis 9:18-27].

And those same preachers also quoted the Christian Scriptures. They reminded the slaves that the Apostle Paul converted a slave to Christianity one time, but he had not freed the man; he sent the slave back to his master [Philemon1:12].

Yes, for over 200 years slave-owners in America used Holy Scripture as a weapon before the Civil War to control slaves – and for the next 100 years the white majority did the same thing, even after slavery was abolished.

Can you imagine what African Americans must have felt like? Can you imagine what it would be like to be told over and over again that it is God's desire for you to be a slave because in antiquity your foreparents sinned – and now you and all your children are cursed forever. You talk about giving someone an inferiority complex!

Then, imagine that even the common language is even used against you by the dominant culture. In those days, it was commonplace for the majority of Americans to use words – horrible, painful, spiteful words – that were used to turn African Americans into labels instead of human beings created in the image of a loving God.

And in the mist of all that societal and spiritual oppression, I believe God raised up African American women and men who somehow did not believe the lies being told them. God raised up people in the African American community to lead their people out of slavery and into freedom. That community learned a Divine Truth from Christian Scriptures: "And we who have been baptized into union with Christ are enveloped by Him. We are no longer Jews or Greeks or slaves or free people or even women or men, but we are all the same – we are Christian; we are one in Christ Jesus. And if you are Christ's, then you are Abraham and Sarah's offspring, heirs according to promise." [Galatians 3:27-29]

The same truth that our sisters and brothers in the African American community learned must be taught to all people. God did not create anybody so God could have someone to hate!

For example, in the lesbian and gay community of which I am a member, I still meet people who believe God hates them because of their sexual orientation. Like the African American community, we have been taught lies about ourselves by the dominant culture. We have been told that we are an "abomination" to God, that the Holy Scriptures condemn homosexuality and that we who profess to be Christians must become heterosexual if we are going to Heaven.

I was taught that lie by my culture. And I accepted that lie as the truth until the day I was forced to look inside myself to find who I really am. And what did I discover?

Let me share this part of my journey.

You see, I have been a homosexual all my life for as long as I can remember.

But a turning point in my life came one day when I was 25 years of age. On that day, I took a long look at myself while standing in front of a mirror in the bathroom of the parsonage of the church where I pastored in Santa Ana, California.

Three days before, I had walked into a bookstore to purchase a magazine which contained an article I intended to use in a sermon.

That visit to that bookstore to buy that magazine changed my life.

When I walked up to the cash register to pay for it, my eye caught some male physique magazines. Well, I paused and looked at them. I could never even remember having seen any physique magazines in my life. I paused and browsed. I really looked at those books. I was really interested in them!

I was there so long I was too embarrassed to leave, and too embarrassed to buy them. Finally, I realized I was being stared at by the management. So I went up to the woman behind the counter, and said to her, "Tell me something. Do you have any books on homosexuality?" Believe me, at the time that was a hard word for me to get out.

She was very courteous. She smiled at me, and said, "Yes, we do have a few."

So I gathered my courage and said, "Well, give me a copy of everything you've got."

She sold me a package of paperbacks and magazines, and I wrote out a check for them. I took the bag of reading matter home, and in the quietness of the parsonage, I started reading – really studying. I read "The Homosexual In America" by Donald Webster Cory. There was a magazine the woman had dropped into the bag called "ONE," and it was published by One, Incorporated, one of the oldest homophile organizations in America. As I read, I discovered there were millions of other homosexuals all across

America just like me. And as I continued reading, a burden seemed to lift from my shoulders. I would set the books and magazines aside and think awhile, and then I'd pick them back up and re-read them. Finally, I read Cory's book and "ONE" for a third time.

Then I hid them all. I was married and I didn't want my wife to find them.

And now here I was, standing in front of the mirror. For the first time in my life I really looked at myself deep inside.

"Troy Perry, you're a homosexual," I said out loud. A burden was gone instantly. I started crying, but these were tears of joy. I had found the answer. The answer was found in acceptance and affirmation! I had discovered my truth.

And then the questions came.

Now I wish I could tell you that was the end of my faith journey and that there and then I accepted myself as a gay Christian.

But that was not the case.

You see, I still believed the lie that my church taught me; the lie that said God hated me because I was a homosexual. For a long time I had repressed my homosexuality – my God-given nature – and I had listened to the lie a very long time. Like the seed of a noxious weed, the lie had sprouted and its roots ran deep into my psyche. It didn't matter that I had been born a homosexual; it didn't matter that I had been a homosexual all my life. The church I grew up in said God hated me and I had accepted that that was all I needed to know.

The Christian culture had made up its mind about me. God's mind was made up about me. At least, that's what I thought.

But thank God I was wrong!

It took almost three more years of wandering in the spiritual wilderness before I was able to hear God tell me what God really thought about me as a gay man.

I went through three years of wandering, searching, pain and struggle – but it was all worthwhile!

First, I was dismissed from my church. Then I separated from my wife. Later I was drafted into the military. After living in Germany for almost two years, I fell in love with another man. But the relationship didn't last. And when he walked out of my life, I thought life was no longer worth living. I didn't want to live. I even tried to kill myself. If my partner couldn't love me and if God couldn't love me, why should I go on living?

From the time I left the church I had felt like a child separated from a family against its will. In my mind, I played and replayed the words of the church officials who harshly told me God couldn't love me because I was gay. (It was only later, as part of my spiritual growth, that I learned God had never, never, never said that. People claiming to represent God put those words in God's mouth – an outgrowth of their own societal biases and prejudices.)

That's when I made a fascinating discovery: accepting that I was gay was not enough. Don't misunderstand me. I believe coming to accept our homosexuality is a vital, indispensable step in growing into wholeness and emotional health.

But for me, a powerful, life-giving component was still missing from my life. I had not addressed the God-given hunger for spirituality – a hunger found in every human being in every culture around the world.

You see, from the point in my life when I accepted myself as a gay male until I picked up a razor blade and cut my wrist, I was spiritually dead. I had taken the attitude "O.K., God; I can't love you and you can't love me so don't bug me and I will not bother you."

I will be eternally grateful that God does not respond to us the same way we respond to God!

My roommate discovered me in the bathroom in the grisly mess I had made. He and our next door neighbors tied up my wrists with cloths and rushed me off to the hospital. By the time I arrived at the emergency room, I was weak and dazed. I hovered between life and death. My heart was racing and my blood pressure was falling. I was really an emotional mess. I didn't know whether I would live or die – and I didn't care.

But I was scared.

If ever I went through a nervous breakdown, that must have been it. I was crying uncontrollably. I did feel painfully human for a change. I cried for more than three hours while waiting for additional medical attention.

Other cases were lined up ahead of me in the emergency room. I was sitting there, crying uncontrollably, when someone walked in front of me and stood there for a minute. I was only vaguely aware of this person, like a shadow before me. This person reached down and stuck a magazine into my hands and said, "Here, some of us care!"

I lifted my head in my weakened condition and stared at this African American woman who softly said, "I don't know why you have done this, but can't you just look up?" It was like a slap in the face. It snapped me out of my despondency, just to hear that someone cared. And then as quickly as she had appeared she was gone. I never knew her name, but I have thanked God for her countless times.

And when she was gone, my thoughts turned to God. I began to talk to God.

I stopped crying. I looked at my bandaged wrists and said, "All right, Lord, I've made some terrible mistakes. You just help me with them."

And I tell you the truth, I felt a weight go out of my life. I had been purged. I felt cleansed. I tell you the truth, before I left that hospital I was alright, perfectly alright. I was as calm and centered as I have ever been.

Finally, the doctors stitched the wounds in my wrists. One doctor came by and said, "There is nothing wrong with you that a swift kick in the ass won't take care of. You know, don't you, that you're too young for this sort of thing?"

So I went home. And the next day I laid in bed thinking about what had happened to me since I had accepted the fact that I am a homosexual. I also thought about my prayer the day before and how good it felt. About how good I felt right then. I was feeling the joy of my salvation!

And then I remembered. "Wait God," I thought. "This can't be you. The Church says you can't love me. I don't know what this wonderful feeling is, but I am still gay. That hasn't changed, so you can't love me!"

As I lay on my bed, God spoke to me. I heard God's still small voice – not audibly – but clearly in my mind. It was as clear and real as any experience in my life.

I heard God's voice say, "Troy, don't tell me what I can and can't do. I love you. You are my son. I don't have stepsons and stepdaughters!"

I knew at that moment, I was God's child. I knew without a doubt I could be a Christian and a gay man. I would never doubt again.

God did not create me so God could have someone to hate!

I knew that all my gay and lesbian and bisexual and transgender sisters and brothers are created in the image and likeness of God. God breathed the breath of life into our bodies. God made us living, immortal souls.

In that moment, I was forever persuaded that no human being can take away God's love for me. No matter what lie they bring against me, no matter what words they try to use to reduce me to being a label instead of a person, no matter what Scripture they misquote, take out of context, or misinterpret. I know that God loves me just the way I am!

We are on a journey – a journey that takes us from our past into the future. But the journey is lived out in the present. When we discover who God created us to be, there is joy, celebration, and self-affirmation.

As you continue on your journey, know that God didn't create you so God could have someone to sit around and hate!

CHAPTER TWO
GOD ALWAYS MAKES ROOM FOR THE EXCEPTION

I know something about you.

In fact, though I may not know you well – I know something deeply, intensely personal about you. In fact, I know at least two things about you.

First, you have a deep, intense hunger for love.

And, second, I know that the God of the Universe – the God who flung stars and moons and galaxies into the farthest recesses of outer space – the God of All Creation loves you.

That's right. Every human being – regardless of their faith or culture or status or education or gender – has an inborn need to find love... and to know they are loved by God.

This need is the ultimate search of the soul for acceptance.

I know something else from 35 years of ministry to people from every walk of life: If you do not reach a deep and personal understanding that the God of the Universe loves you, the odds are that you will wander though life in a spiritual void that will impact every area of your existence in the most profound ways.

Now that's a heavy thought! And it sets most of us up for another problem.

You see, almost all humans who live today have been told at one time or another by some individual or group of people, whether religious or not, that they are not loved by God.

Individuals and religious groups who practice this Satanic Art of Judging others are responsible for the genocide of millions of people in history. In fact, if we are honest with ourselves, this genocide is not due to religion so much as it is due to the Satanic Art of Judging.

Human beings around the world – in all cultures and in every age – have been put to death, have been told they were going to die and go to hell, and have been excommunicated – simply for disagreeing with the interpretation of Holy Scripture by people who claim to speak for God.

Now, it is not my desire to belittle the spiritual beliefs of anyone. But here is a list of just a few acts that various churches and Christian denominations have taught in the past, or are still teaching today are sins which can send you to hell:

> **Eating meat on Friday; believing the sun was the center of the universe; marrying a person of another faith; reading and owning a Bible; dancing; drinking alcohol; women cutting their hair; going to movie theaters; wearing of jewelry for ornamentation or decoration; singing in church accompanied by a musical instrument; using Sunday as the Lords Day instead of Saturday; use of medicine by clergy, and women wearing pants; men wearing neckties; saluting a flag; participating in the affairs of government; bearing arms in war; receiving a blood transfusion; jesting; the use of slang; attending Church Sunday schools; use of armed force; driving automobiles; divorce and remarriage of clergy; women preaching in church.**

I am sorry to say that all of these were taught by Christian denominations and Christian churches. Since I am a Christian minister I have kept the list to my faith. I could go on and on with other religious groups and the standards they have imposed as "sins," but I think you've got the idea.

My point is you do not have to be a homosexual to be told, "You're going to hell."

One of the things I have grown to love most about God is God's creative ability to keep human beings from boxing God in. Human nature wants to confine God and control people. True spirituality liberates both!

Just when we think we know all there is to know about God, God does a new thing. that's because God always makes room for the exception!

Just as the Radical Religious Right in the U.S.A. has tried to be the only voice of God in our age, people in the past have tried the same thing. Listen to me: The prophets of the popular culture are not necessarily prophets of the living God!

You need look no further than the Bible. Ancient prophets and patriarchs boasted, "We have kept all the Law of God, we have done all for God."

But God replied, "My thoughts are not your thoughts, my ways are not your ways." (Isaiah 55:8)

Wow! Did you let that sink into your being? God says God's ways are not the ways of humans... and certainly God's ways are not the ways of oppressive religious leaders!

I have learned over the years in reading and studying Sacred Scripture that you can change the mind of God. Both the Hebrew and Christian Scripture give us examples of God saying God was going to do one thing, but then doing something else. There is a spiritual principal here: God is always willing to make room for the exception.

And (the Religious Right won't tell you this, but) we also have examples of God changing the spiritual laws that had been proclaimed in God's name.

Let me give you a great example.

One of the most famous stories taught in many church Sunday Schools is the story of Jonah and the Whale found in the Hebrew Scriptures (see the Book of Jonah).

In this well-known story, God tells Jonah to deliver a message to the people in the ancient Middle Eastern city of Nineveh. The message is simple and direct: In forty days God will destroy their city. The King of Nineveh believes what Jonah has said. So he calls for his kingdom to pray and fast. And when God sees the people turn from their evil ways, the Hebrew writer of the Book of Jonah says, "God saw their works, that they turned from their evil way; and God repented of the evil that God had said would be done to them; and God did it not." [Jonah 3: 10]

The people responded to God's message, and God's mind was changed. God always makes room for the exception!

Here's another great illustration from the Bible. In the Book of Leviticus in the Hebrew Scriptures, God gives the prophet a law describing how the Children of Israel are to make animal sacrifices.

God is to receive burnt offerings – and Yahweh (one of the sacred Hebrew names for God) does for hundreds of years. And then Yahweh's mind is changed.

Along comes a Hebrew prophet by the name of Isaiah. He delivers a new prophecy to the Children of Israel. The prophecy, as it has come down to us, begins with a lament that is highly unflattering to the people of the ancient Hebrew covenant: "Israel knows nothing, my people understand nothing." Ouch!

Yahweh had become utterly revolted by the animal sacrifices, sickened by the sacrificial, ceremonial blood of bulls and goats and the reeking odor of the sacrificial smoke. God had grown tired of people following external rituals and rules when their hearts were far from God and God's ways. (This becomes one of the great themes of the Scriptures: Humans judge by external actions and signs, but God looks upon our hearts.)

So Yahweh let the people know, through the prophet Isaiah, that external observance was not enough. The people of the covenant must discover the inner meaning of their religion. Yahweh wanted compassion rather than sacrifice: "When you make many prayers, I will not hear you: your hands are full of blood. Wash and make yourself clean; put away the evil of your doings from before mine eyes; cease to do evil; learn to do what is right; seek judgment, relieve the oppressed, judge the fatherless, plead for the widow." [Isaiah 1:15-17]

Let me give you another illustration to build my case:

When God gave the Ten Commandments [see Exodus 20:1-17] to Moses, only one was a "sex sin" that under Hebrew law called for the death penalty [Leviticus 20:10] –

the sin of adultery. If you committed adultery you were to be stoned to death. For hundreds of years that's what happened.

And then Jesus came and changed everything! God had a new message for humankind, a message filled with spiritual irony: "Only people who are perfect and do not sin may stone others to death." [see the Gospel of John 8:3-11] I believe Jesus' words ended the use of the death penalty by human beings once and for all since none of us is "without sin."

"You are going to hell for that" is one of the oldest phrases ever used by human beings. It is as old as humankind itself. We humans love judgment. We really do love to be legalistic – to impose our rules and standards and judgment.

From my study of the Christian Scriptures I learned that the only people Jesus ever used that phrase with were judgmental, legalistic, religious, self-righteous hypocrites. Jesus described hypocrites this way: "This people honors me with their lips, but their heart is far from me; in vain do they worship me, teaching as doctrines the precepts of men." [Matthew 15:8-9]

It's interesting to note that during his earthly existence, Jesus was constantly questioned by religious hypocrites. They not only questioned him, they loved to accuse him. They accused him of not living by the ancient spiritual laws and of breaking the spiritual laws. They called him evil, a blasphemer, and demon possessed.

I know the feeling.

During my 30 years of ministry in the lesbian and gay

community I have been called all of the above – and more!

Why did religious hypocrites hate Jesus so much? It was because Jesus knew a divine truth: God always makes room for the exception!

The religious hypocrites of Jesus' day were controlling. They thought they had all the answers. The placed God in a box; they saw God as rigid and unbending. Into their midst comes Jesus, who teaches that God transcends limitations and situations and makes exceptions to our limited human understanding.

(Why do religious hypocrites today hate God's gay and lesbian children so much? Same reason; same divine truth: Because God always makes room for the exception – and gay men and lesbians are, from the view of the dominant culture, exceptions to society's norms!)

Here's a profound thought that's worth thinking about: Jesus knew it's harder to die and go to hell than we have been taught.

That's true! But religious hypocrites do not want you to know that. They want everyone to believe that only they are going to get to heaven – and that they get to decide who else will be there with them.

They hated Jesus because he dared to give them a new commandment – a liberating commandment – that was not like the old law at all!

"You shall love the Lord your God with all your heart, and with all your soul, and with all your intellect. This is the great and first commandment. And the second is like it, You shall love your neighbor as you do yourself. These two commandments sum up God's Law and upon these depends all the Law and the prophets." [Matthew 22:37-40]

The Scriptures are filled with teachings about love: God is love. We are to love one another. We are to reflect God's love to our world. We are to live our lives with love.

See, Jesus knew another truth: God has always loved you – just as you are! In Psalm 22:10 declares, "From my mother's womb thou has been my God" and Isaiah 44:2 says, "You [God] fashioned me from birth." Before your birth, God loved you! Even before the creation of the world, God knew when you would arrive on the earth... what you would be like... what your sexual orientation would be... what your physical and personal characteristics would be. And God loved you. Just as you are.

All that God desires is that you love in return.

Cultural prophets tell me that as a gay male I must ask God for deliverance from my homosexuality if I am to be a member of the Christian faith. What they really believe is that I must become a heterosexual before I can pray to "receive the faith." The cultural prophet's error is to believe that God expects all human beings to marry heterosexually or at least to be heterosexual if they choose to be single.

Wrong! Here again God makes room for the exception.

God taught me a divine truth over 30 years ago concerning the lesbian and gay community (and everybody else).

You are made in the image of God and you do not owe apologies to any human being for that!

When the ancient Scriptures were written, God used two

metaphors – two word pictures – to speak to our community. The first is "barren women" and the second is "male eunuchs." Now, those words may sound outdated and antiquated – but when you study and understand them in the context of the ancient Hebrew civilization, you discover that God has filled the Bible with a message of hope for lesbians, gay men, bisexuals and transgender persons!

In the ancient Hebrew civilization, both of these classes of individuals – barren women and male eunuchs – were viewed as being outside of the norm of the culture. They both were viewed as rejecting the commandment of God to "be fruitful and multiply." Something was wrong.

People talked about them... judged them. They wondered: "Had they sinned or had their parents sinned for them to be in this condition?" It just wasn't natural. They were considered to be "out of the will of God." Evidently, these people couldn't or wouldn't have children, so people in that culture assumed that God loved them less.

Ancient cultures viewed barren women as unable to fulfill the plan of God for women in general. Here is their error:

They took one thing they believed God said and turned that word into an idol.

When the children of Israel left the bondage of Egypt for the liberation of the Promised Land, God said they would be given a new land where, "nothing will miscarry, nor be barren." [Exodus 23:26] and again, "You shall be blessed above all people: there shall not be male or female barren among you, or among your cattle." [Deuteronomy 7:14]

To be a barren woman in ancient Israel – to be unable to

bear children – was bad news indeed! (And the Radical Religious Right is still trying to use this old lie to justify their denunciation of lesbians today.)

Now, a word about male eunuchs. Eunuchs were blamed for their condition even though they had not created their condition. But because they were eunuchs, they could not be priests of God. In fact, they were even prohibited from placing their gifts on God's alter.

Now all this was justified by the law of that time. The message for barren women and male eunuchs was clear; if you couldn't marry and you couldn't have children, you did not fit into the family of God.

Ah, but remember the spiritual principle: God always makes room for the exception!

God grew tired of the children of Israel believing that old lie and sent a prophet to correct their understanding of the truth: "I'm going to upset the lie you've tried to make into the truth. I'm going to add the people you hold as outcasts to my divine family."

"Thus says the Lord, Keep judgment, and do justice: for my salvation is near to come, and my righteousness to be revealed. Blessed is the person that does this, and their children that lay hold on it; that keeps the Sabbath from polluting it, and keeps their hand from doing any evil. Neither let the children of the stranger, that has joined themselves to the Lord, speak, saying, The Lord has utterly separated me from his people: neither let the eunuch say, Behold I am unable to have children.

For thus says the Lord unto the eunuch (and everyone else) that keep my Sabbaths, and choose the things that please me, and take hold of my covenant; Even unto them will I give in my house and within my walls a place and a name better than of sons and of daughters: I will give them an everlasting name, that shall not be cut off.

Also the children of the stranger, that join themselves to the Lord to serve God, and to love the name of the Lord, to be God's servants, every one that keeps the Sabbath from polluting it, and takes hold of my covenant;

Even them will I bring to my holy mountain, and make them joyful in my house of prayer: their burnt offerings and their sacrifices shall be accepted upon my altar; for my house shall be called a house of prayer for all people." [Isaiah 56:1-8]

Still some people didn't get the message.

Then, on to the human stage stepped Jesus. Jesus came to show us new ways of looking at life. Jesus always delighted in the exception!

One day Jesus was teaching his disciples. Interestingly enough, Jesus used a discourse on heterosexual marriage to proclaim another divine truth: Not everyone is born heterosexual. Surprise!

"Not everyone can accept this statement," Jesus said. "Only those whom God helps. For there are eunuchs who have been born incapable of (heterosexual) marriage, and there are eunuchs who have been made so by man, and there are eunuchs who have made themselves eunuchs for the sake of the dominion of heaven. Let anyone who is able to receive this, receive it." [Matthew 19:11-12]

Do you get the message? What Jesus is saying is that not

all human beings are born with a heterosexual orientation. I was born a homosexual and my homosexuality is a gift of God. To try to be anything other than that for me would be a sin. Remember, no matter what human thinking may be, God always makes room for the exception!

I want to use one more example of this divine truth.

Among the profound research that has taken place in the 20th Century has been greater attention to studying ways the Christian Faith became the Christian Church it is today.

From this research, we've learned the Christian Church has made centuries of mistakes by filtering the Hebrew Scriptures through later Christian beliefs. But the only way to discover truth in the Hebrew Scriptures is to understand it in terms of the Hebrew language, Hebrew culture, and Hebrew traditions. When we impose our later Christian understanding on the Hebrew Scriptures (the first part of the Bible from Genesis through the writing of the Hebrew prophet Malachi), we will invariably reach wrong conclusions. And that's exactly what the Radical Religious Right has done with the Bible!

We understand today that the early Christian Believers thought of themselves as a continuing part of the Jewish faith. We tend to forget that they continued to worship in the Temple in Jerusalem and attended services at local synagogues because all of the early converts to the Christian faith were Jews just as Jesus was. (I like to point out to people that Jesus was a Jew who never attended a Christian Church.)

The earliest Christians continued to observe the Jewish law. They thought of themselves as part of the Jewish main stream and they were until two things happened.

First, the biblical character Saul, who would later be called Paul (St. Paul), was converted to the Christian faith, and second, Peter (St. Peter), an apostle of the Christian faith, had a vision that revealed a powerful, life-changing, life-affirming truth about God.

We have to remember that members of the Jewish faith were people born into families that were part of the Children of Israel. The only exception to the rule were individuals who requested to convert to the Jewish faith and kept its law. These converts were small in number as the Jewish faith did not proselytize. According to the Jewish faith, people who were not part of the Children of Israel were called "Gentiles." The one thing that every male Jewish convert had to undertake to become a new member of the Jewish faith was the act of circumcision. In the Jewish religion, this outward symbol identified those who were Jewish – and separated them from those who were Gentiles.

Now, the apostle Peter was one of the first believers of the Christian faith. He received his spiritual call from Jesus and became the first follower of the small group of individuals who followed Jesus during his earthly existence. This group is often referred to as the Disciples, or the Apostles. [Matthew 4:18-19]

Peter watched the earliest beginnings of Jesus' ministry on earth, and lived and traveled with him until Jesus' death. Peter was a witness to the resurrection of Christ and proclaimed it to the early Christian believers.

Peter quickly became one of the pillars of the early Christian community. Peter was the charismatic leader of the Christian faith in Jerusalem. He helped organize the first Jewish Christians into their own Christian synagogue, which he called a church. By the way, this only happened after the larger

Jewish community rejected the Christian Jews' belief that Jesus was "God in the flesh, the Promised One, the Messiah." Even so, these believers continued to worship as fully observant Jews.

And then God intervened in history. God again made room for the exception. The story is told in the Book of The Acts of the Apostles in Christian Scriptures.

A Roman centurion who received the gift of the Holy Spirit almost caused the death of the early Christian church. [Acts 10]

You see, Cornelius, was not only a centurion, but also a Gentile. According to Christian Scripture, Cornelius was "a devout man, and one that feared God with all his house, which gave much alms to the people, and prayed to God always."

As he prayed one day something wonderful happened to him. He clearly saw a vision of an angel of God entering his home and greeting him. Gazing intently at the angel, he became frightened.

He then said, "What is it, God?"

And the angel said to him, "Your prayers and your generous gifts to the poor have not gone unnoticed by God! Now send some servants to the city of Joppa to find a man named Simon Peter, who is staying with Simon the Tanner, down by the shore, and ask him to come and visit with you. He has a message to share with you."

While that was happening to Cornelius, God was preparing to visit the apostle Peter. The following day it was Peter's turn to receive a vision.

While the men sent by Cornelius were approaching the town, Peter went up on the roof of the house to pray. It was noon. He was hungry and wanted something to eat; while the meal was being prepared he fell into a spiritual trance.

In this trance, or vision, Peter saw the sky open, and a great canvas sheet suspended by its four corners settled to the ground. In the sheet were all the animals that Jews were forbidden to eat according to the Hebrew Scriptures in the book of Leviticus. (These particular animals were considered to be unclean for dietary purposes; they were not kosher.) And there, while in the trance, a voice speaks. "Rise, Peter; kill and eat."

"Never, Lord," declared Peter, "they are forbidden by our Jewish law. I have never in all my life eaten such creatures."

The voice spoke again, "Don't contradict God! If God says something is kosher, then it is!"

Now, this unusual occurrence was repeated three times. Then immediately the sheet was taken up to heaven. To say that Peter was inwardly perplexed by the interpretation of the vision would be an understatement. But just then the messengers sent by Cornelius arrived. Even as Peter was thinking and puzzled about the vision, the Spirit of God said to Peter again, "Three men have come to see you. Go down and meet them and go with them. All is well, I have sent them."

So Peter went down to greet the visitors. "I am the one you are looking for," he said, "What do you want?"

The messengers rapidly told Peter everything about Cornelius and the vision he had from God telling him to invite Peter to his home. "He has received an answer to prayer a warning to listen to and act upon what you have to say," the men said.

So Peter leaves the city of Joppa with the messengers and some Jewish Christian believers. After a day's travel they arrive at the home of Cornelius.

Cornelius, in the meantime, had invited many of his relatives and his intimate friends to be with him when the apostle of God arrived to share the message the angel has promised.

Well, the meeting got off to a bad start. Upon meeting Peter, Cornelius falls down at Peter's feet and made obeisance and paid worshipful reverence to Peter. But Peter helps him to his feet and says, "Get up, I myself am also human." They talked together for a while as Peter tried to get his nerves together and then went in to where the others were assembled.

Peter told them, "You know it is against the Jewish law for me to come into a Gentile home like this. But God has shown me in a vision that I should never think of anyone as being common, or unclean, or inferior. Therefore, I came. But tell me what do you want?"

Cornelius told Peter in his own words of his vision and the angels words.

"You have a message for me from God. Tell me what it is," said Cornelius.

Peter said, "I see very clearly that the Jews are not God's only favorites! In every nation God has those who worship God and do good deeds and are acceptable to God."

Peter then delivered a powerful, life-changing message. He shared with them the wonderful story of Jesus, the Christ. It is the story of Jesus' life, death, resurrection, and the fact that everyone who believes in Christ will have their sins forgiven through His name.

Now, in the middle of his message Peter lost control of the meeting. Without warning the Spirit of God took over and Cornelius and his entire household received the gift of spiritual salvation. These uncircumcised Gentiles received the power and presence of the Holy Spirit and responded with the same evidence that the Jewish Christians demonstrated in the Jerusalem Church! The Jewish Christians who had come with Peter were surprised and amazed.

Then Peter asked, "Can anyone forbid or refuse water for baptizing these people, seeing that they have received the Holy Spirit just as we have?" And he ordered that they be baptized in the name of Jesus Christ, the Messiah.

Again, God made room for the exception!

When the members at First Church in Jerusalem heard God had given the Gentiles the presence and power of the Holy Spirit just like them, they were thrilled!

Right? Wrong!

There is something in human nature that becomes comfortable with life's ruts – and that resists change, even positive change. that's always been true with institutional, organized religion.

In fact, I'm fond of saying that the "Seven Last Words of the Church" have always been, "We've never done it this way before."

Well, the church members in First Church in Jerusalem were upset!

"What do you mean you baptized a bunch of uncircumcised gentiles and were a guest in their home? Don't you know what the Scriptures say?" they asked.

You see, fundamentalism was alive and well in ancient Israel!

Peter reiterated the story of his vision, describing the message God had given him. "How could I have not done what I did after God said to do it?" Peter asked.

The story in the Book of Acts in the Christian Scriptures reads, "When the believers heard this, all their objections were answered." [Acts 11:18a]

So was that the end of the story?

Well, not quite. A fight broke out!

"Well, okay," the early church said. "The Gentiles can become Christians, but they must also follow the Jewish law and become Jewish by being circumcised."

Now, this is the same argument that the Radical Religious Right continues to use against the lesbian and gay community in our day. They say, "Yes, you can become a Christian, but you also must become a heterosexual."

Into this mess walks another saint of the early church, the Apostle Paul.

Paul was a convert to the Christian faith who came to the faith after Jesus died. He became the greatest missionary of the early church. He traveled into almost all the known world of his time. He was also a Roman citizen even though he was a Jew.

He had a passion for the Gospel of Jesus Christ and a passion for sharing it with all people he met. As he became a pillar of the Christian faith, he became one of the most prolific writers of letters to the early church. These letters were known as "epistles," and many became books of the Bible. Paul believed he was an apostle. Even though he had not been elected to the position by the other apostles after the death of Judas, he believed he had been called to the position by the Spirit of God.

When Paul heard of the vision of Peter, he began to preach the liberating gospel to the Gentiles with a passion.

Some time later Paul and another leader in the Christian community, Barnabas, established a church in the ancient city of Antioch. While they were there, some Christian followers came to visit the church from Judea. They instructed the believers, "Unless you are circumcised in accordance with the Mosaic custom, you cannot find spiritual salvation." [Acts 15]

Sound familiar?

It was the same old argument all over again.

Paul, Barnabas and some other members of the Antioch Church went to Jerusalem to meet with the Apostles and Elders to discuss the matter.

And once again Peter retells the story of the vision he received from God. And again the Apostles and the church in Jerusalem reaffirmed the doctrine that Gentile believers of the Christian faith did not have to be circumcised to become Jews in order to also become Christians.

Now, what does all of this have to do with you?

As a minister of God, I share the truth revealed to me by the Holy Spirit:

You do not have to be or become a heterosexual in order to be a convert of the Christian faith.

Only one thing is required: Your acceptance of Jesus Christ as your Savior and Sovereign. Period.

God has made you kosher, because God always makes room for the exception!

CHAPTER THREE
THE LORD IS MY SHEPHERD AND KNOWS WHAT I AM!

God knows everything there is to know about Troy Perry.

And God knows everything there is to know about you.

God knows our every thought and action. God knew us in our mother's womb. God has seen us at our best and our worst and for some reason God deeply loves us. We, every one of us, are made in the image of God. We are the apple of God's eye.

Throughout my ministry, God has reminded me again and again, that God knew what I was even before my birth. God reminds me I am a homosexual because that's the way God wanted me to be. My homosexuality is a gift from God.

I have four younger brothers and I have learned that their heterosexuality is God's gift to them. My family makes no apologies to each other for these wonderful and different gifts God has given each of us. After all, is it any wonder that the same God who created such a rich tapestry of diversity on this planet would also create a diversity of sexualities?

Because my homosexuality is an innate gift from God, I embrace and proclaim two lessons. First, I cannot change from being what I was created to be. Second, because my sexuality is a God given gift, I would not want to change. Embracing these two lessons is a sign of emotional and spiritual health.

Think about it:

Why would we ever conform to society's expectations at the expense of God's plan for our lives?

Given those two choices, God's plan for your life will also be far more rewarding and fulfilling than the standards imposed by the popular culture.

I am always saddened when I meet a member of the lesbian and gay community who believes the lie that God wants them to change their sexual orientation. After thirty years of ministry in the GLBT communities, I tell you, it cannot be done.

Twenty two years ago, a young man began to attend Metropolitan Community Church in Los Angeles, California. I served as the senior minister. He came to see me with a question. Before he would ask me the question, though, he told me a story that was both funny and sad.

Jim shared with me that six weeks before our meeting his partner, John, had received a telephone call from his sister in North Carolina. She had been thinking about him and wanted to come to California to visit him. Being a loving, caring brother, he told her he would love to see her and invited her to California for a visit.

"Well, surprise," she said. "I am in California, and I'll be over shortly."

John hung up the phone. And panicked!

"Oh my God! My sister Pat is coming here! She's very conservative and very religious. And she doesn't know that I'm gay or that I'm in a relationship with a man!" John said.

"And I don't want her to know. It would cause major problems with my family."

Well, the sister arrived. And Jim and John went through an elaborate charade. They put Pat in their guest bedroom – but pretended that it was John's bedroom, as though they were two heterosexual roommates. John then slept on the couch.

Got the picture?

Now, Jim didn't like this arrangement one bit, but he went along with the charade to keep peace in John's family.

"Everything was fine until three days ago. I hadn't slept with John for over a week," Jim said, "and I couldn't stand it anymore. I woke up and heard John in the kitchen cooking breakfast. I got up, dressed, and slipped down the hall into the kitchen. I slipped up behind John and gave him a great big hug and a kiss on the back of the neck. And at that very moment, Pat walked into the room."

"I thought something like this was going on!" shrieked Pat."You know better than this, John, even if Jim doesn't. You attended Bob Jones University where they teach Christian fundamentalism. You've been taught the truth. Homosexuality is a sin and you know it!"

"Right then and there, Pat demanded we pray. I didn't know what to do; everything felt so awkward. No sooner was the prayer finished than she started quoting verses out of the Bible. She told us that if weren't delivered from our homosexuality we would die and go to hell. She even laid hands on John and rebuked the demon of homosexuality."

"God sent me here to rescue you from this sin and to take

you back home with me," Pat said. "Pack up, John, God has delivered you."

"I was totally shocked by this whole scene. But imagine my added shock, Rev. Perry, when John told her that, yes, he was going home with her and that he had been delivered from his homosexuality."

"And Rev. Perry, they left this morning. Rev. Perry, I was raised in a Roman Catholic family and I can quote the catechism front and back, but I don't use scripture as a weapon like you Protestants do."

"What does God want of me?" he asked. "Does God want me to change? And do you think I will see John again?"

Does God want me to change? During 30 years of ministry in the lesbian, gay, bisexual and transgender communities, I have been asked that very question hundreds of times.

I certainly remember asking that question to God myself. And God answered, "Yes and no."

I thought, "What kind of answer is that, God? Make up your mind, yes or no."

And God spoke to me again, "Yes and no."

Is my basic sexual orientation able to change? In the Bible, God frequently asks questions which also make powerful statements. In the Hebrew Scriptures, God speaks through the Prophet Jeremiah and asks this question: "Can the Ethiopian change the color of the skin, or the leopard its spots?" [The Book of the Prophet Jeremiah 13:23]

Now, the answer is rather obvious, isn't it? With only a moment's thought, you know the answer. The answer to both questions is "No."

If you're like me though, you do notice human beings sure love to try.

In this day of cosmetic surgery, tinted contact lenses, hair color, and makeup, people certainly try!

I love to point out to members of our church that we can pray for anything, but it does not mean God is going answer that prayer the way we want. We can pray all day, "God, I hate the color of my hair. I hear blondes have more fun. Please, dear God, make me a blonde!"

Let me be perfectly candid with you. God is not going to answer that prayer.

But, one day you wake up and discover that you can change the color of your hair by buying a box of hair coloring. So you buy the product, follow the procedures – and become the most flamboyant platinum blonde in Hollywood! And look what happens. Your friends start telling you how good you look and before long you could even conceivably deceive yourself into believing you were born a natural blonde.

But if you don't keep using the product, we'll soon be seeing your real color at the roots.

Or, one day you are looking in the mirror and you say, "God, I hate these brown eyes of mine. They don't go with my new blonde hair. Please, dear God, give me big blue eyes." Again, you can pray until you are blue in the face, but that won't translate into blue in your eyes! Simply put,

God is not going to answer that prayer. So buy tinted contact lenses. You buy a pair that are so blue that every time you look at someone they think you're from the "Village of the Damned!" Again, you can wear them until you begin to believe you have blue eyes, but every time you take them out, you will see the brown eyes you were born with.

Here's my point: We human beings can superficially change anything, but that does not mean that anything has really changed at a deep, profound, significant level.

My heart is saddened when I meet lesbians and gay males who are caught in the web of fear and guilt created by the Radical Religious Right, or by some well-meaning but misguided person trying to tell the lesbian or gay individual that God can change them from being homosexual. Listen to me: That is a Satanic lie!

All of the current research shows that, just like your hair color or your eye color, so too, your sexual orientation is innate and inborn. Your sexual orientation is a gift from God. Rejoice and be thankful for it.

I can honestly tell you, I have never met one person who has ever changed their sexual orientation by prayer, meditation, therapy, psychology or any other means. God doesn't require it and people can't make it happen.

God's creation is good! And that includes you!

Remember, the Lord is your shepherd and knows what you are!

One day I was shopping in Los Angeles, where I live. My spouse and I had just walked out of a department store when we noticed a young man looking at me. He came over and asked if I was Rev. Troy Perry. The way he said it sounded more like an accusation than a question. His body language told me he was not a happy camper.

"Yes, that's me," I said smiling.

"Well I've got something to say to you," said he. "There aren't any homosexuals going to heaven!"

As he spun around and walked away from me, I replied, "No heterosexuals are going either."

What?

Well, you see, the Christian Scriptures teach me that our sexual orientation is not going to heaven with us. In fact, this is taught by most religions in the world. I know this will disappoint some of you, but we won't be labeled heterosexual or homosexual in heaven. (Don't worry. I am convinced that everything in heaven will be on such a higher plane, involving new senses and experiences, that everything about it will be far superior to things on this earthly plane.)

Jesus was once asked a question by a self-righteous know-it-all. This person knew that Jesus believed in an afterlife, that death was not the end of our existence. The questioner did not believe in an afterlife, so he asked Jesus a religious question to trap Jesus. "Sir, Moses said that if a man died without children, his brother should marry the widow and their children would get all the dead man's property. Well, there was among us a family of seven brothers. The first married, and died, and having no children left his wife to his brother. She became the second brother's wife. This brother also died with no children, and the woman was passed on to the next brother, and so on until she had been married to each of them. And then she died. In the resurrection (in heaven) which of the seven brothers will be her husband?"

Jesus said to the man, "After the resurrection (in heaven) they neither marry nor are given in marriage."

Again, Jesus knew a divine truth, there will be no sexual orientation in heaven or hell.

And to answer the question one more time: No, God does not require you to change that part of your personality; that is God's wonderful gift to you. There is a great verse in the Christian Scriptures which declares, "The gifts and the calling of God are without repentance." This simply means that when God gives you a gift – including your sexuality – that's one area where God's mind never changes.

I heard a story once about wanting to change to be something you are not, and its aftermath.

Two little girls lived next door to each other. One, a Caucasian, watched the television news for weeks on end at the beginning of the civil rights movement in America. It was the early 1960's, and the little girl became enthralled with the rapid progress being made by African Americans in the larger culture. One day she visited her African American neighbor, Nancy, and said to the little girl, "I want to join in the fight for civil rights. I want to be black just like you. Can I change?"

"Yes, you can," her little friend said. With that she took her little white neighbor into her parents' garage, took a can of black spray paint, and painted her from head to toe.

When the little white girl saw her change in a mirror, she

was thrilled! She felt an identification with her African American friend.

So she rushed home to share the change with her family. She ran breathlessly up to her mother's bedroom.

"Mother, look at me," the little girl cried triumphantly.

Her mother turned, looked at her daughter in shock. "My God, what have you done?" she screamed. "Go to your father right now and let him see you."

The little girl turned and started back down the stairs when she ran into her brother. Before she could say one word, her brother moved out of her way and said, "Don't touch me. Wait until Dad sees you."

Her father hearing the commotion walked to the bottom of the stairs and saw his daughter.

"Lord," shouted her father. "What in the name of the Saints have you got on you. You go to your room right now young lady. You'll have no dinner tonight until your mother and I can find some way to get that mess off of you!"

Little Sandy went to her bedroom. She sat thinking for about fifteen minutes when the telephone ring and her friend, Nancy, was on the line.

"Well, how are you doing," Nancy asked.

"I can tell you one thing, "Sandy said, "I've only been black for fifteen minutes, and already I've learned to hate whites."

There is one change God desires of each of us: to love.

become Christ-like.

Ever since my childhood, I have always known that God loved me. But it was not until I reached adulthood that I began to understand the depths of God's love for all of us.

Those of us who come from a Christian tradition frequently use the word "salvation." Or we talk about being "saved." Now, popular religions have added lots of negative baggage to this wonderful concept.

In the Bible, "salvation" is used to express a close relationship with the God of the Universe. The Christian Scriptures teach that this relationship is established by embracing the life, teachings, death and resurrection of Jesus. (Please note I did not say by embracing a particular church or theology, but rather, in the Divine Person of Jesus Christ.) This Christian salvation results in emotional and spiritual health, freedom from guilt and doubt, self-acceptance and a deep sense of peace and purpose.

In true Christian theology, "salvation" is always coupled with the word "grace." Grace is a way of saying that salvation comes as a free gift from the God of the Universe. It cannot be bought or earned. Like any generous gift, it is simply to be accepted and embraced.

The reason I can declare with conviction my salvation as a member of the Christian faith is found in Holy Scripture: "If you shall confess with your lips that Jesus Christ is your Sovereign, and believe in your heart that God has raised Jesus from the dead, you will be saved." [The Letter of Paul to the Romans 10:9]

Quite frankly, I am still shocked at the energy that the Radical Religious Right puts into telling people why they are not going to be saved by the grace of God!

There are twin lies that children are taught in too many churches. One is that it is hard to receive salvation from God. The other is that it is hard to hold on to your salvation.

Many leaders in the Radical Religious Right imply that salvation is like candy which they alone have the power to dispense. (Sense the control issues here?)

No religious group, no church, no religious leader, no family, no parent, no angel or demon, no human being – NOBODY! – can keep God's salvation though Jesus Christ from you if you desire it. (that's why the Bible often refers to the message of Christian salvation as the "Good News.") No, all you have to do is ask for it.

I am still amazed at the arrogance of people who tell lesbians, gays, bisexuals and transgender persons that God's Salvation cannot be obtained unless we follow their rules to obtain it.

I have a message for those folks: Your rules don't count!

If I confess with my lips that Jesus is my Sovereign, and believe in my heart that God raised Jesus from the dead, I will be saved! No if's, and's, or but's about it.

I cannot tell you how many times I have had so-called Christians try to tell me why God cannot love me.

Well, here's another message for them: You're too late!

God's already revealed that God knows us from our birth... knows everything about us... and already loves us unconditionally.

I like to remind the naysayers that "The Lord is my light and my salvation; whom shall I fear? The Lord is the strength of my life; of whom shall I be afraid?" [The Book of Psalms 27:1]

Again, the energy I see people expend to try to convince the lesbian and gay community that we cannot be members of the Christian faith if we are "practicing" homosexuals is just beyond me. I often remind folks that it is not the sexual act that makes one homosexual. If I could no longer have sex with anyone anymore, I would still be a homosexual. Not a happy homosexual, but still a homosexual!

The Christian Scriptures tell us, "Whosoever shall call upon the name of Lord shall be saved." [Acts 2:21]

Did you catch that? No limitations. No qualifications. Whosoever! As someone who has been saved and is a Christian, I still ask members of the Radical Religious Right, "What part of "whosoever" don't you understand?

St. John summarized this so powerfully into one sentence when he wrote, "For God so loved the world that God gave God's only begotten Son, that whosoever believes in Jesus should not perish, but shall have everlasting life." [The Gospel according to St. John 3:16]

To members of the lesbian and gay community (and everyone else, too), I just want to remind you that you are a "whosoever" and Christian salvation – with its reality of personal peace, emotional freedom, and message of hope – is yours free for the asking.

God loved you so much that God created you with free will – with the ability to make choices. In creating humanity, God did not want robots, but rather creatures who could think and make choices, including the choice to love. It is God's desire that we love God just as God loves us – unreservedly – but that choice is ours. It is God's desire that we love one another, as we should love ourselves, but again, the choice is ours.

So maybe you're asking, Rev. Perry, how do I obtain this Christian salvation you're talking about?

The way to obtain salvation is simply to talk to God. We Christians call it prayer. A salvation prayer might be, "God, I come to you of my own free will. I ask for the salvation promised to me by you, through the sacrifice of Jesus by his death. I believe you raised Jesus from the dead by the power of God's Spirit. I ask forgiveness for any sins I have committed, intentionally or unintentionally. By faith in your promises, I put my trust in Jesus the Christ and accept your gift of salvation. Amen"

My friend, it's just that simple, but you have to make the choice to talk with God.

Remember, "If we confess our sins, God is faithful and just to forgive us our sins, and to cleanse us from all unrighteousness." [The First Letter of John 1:9]

Yes, then you, too, can truly say, "The Lord is my shepherd and knows who I am!"

CHAPTER FOUR
THE BIBLE IS YOUR FRIEND... NO MATTER WHAT ANYONE SAYS.

I love the Sacred Scriptures which we Christians call the Bible. As a little boy who loved going to Church and Sunday School, I was always excited to learn about the Word of God. Having been raised in a home in which one parent loved the Baptist Church and another the Church of God (Cleveland, Tenn.), I was encouraged to study the Sacred Scriptures. And study them I did.

During the early years of the founding of the Universal Fellowship of Metropolitan Community Churches, when spokespersons for the lesbian and gay community were few and far between, I would end up on radio and television shows debating people who disagreed with my point of view on the subject of homosexuality and the Bible. I don't know why, but they always seemed surprised that an openly gay Christian could know and love the Bible so well.

The other thing I discovered early on was the large number of people in the lesbian and gay community who had been hurt by religious fanatics who used the Bible as a club or weapon. Too many of those fanatics viewed the Bible as something to be feared rather than loved. I have a message for our community: The Bible is your friend no matter what anyone says.

People ask me all the time, "Do you take the Bible literally?"

I always tell them:

"No, I take it seriously."

You see, I believe the Bible is Holy Scripture that was written for all people. I don't believe God ever wanted the Bible to be used for anything other than to carry the "good news" of God's love for all humanity and God's plan for those of us who choose to become believers.

With all my heart, I believe God speaks to the lesbian and gay community (and everyone else, too) through the message of the Bible.

I know from reading the Word of God, that God loves me just the way I am, that I am created in the image of God, and I owe no apologies for being one of God's gay children. I believe the Bible is full of stories that speak to me as a gay man and will speak to you, too, as you read and listen to the wonderful message of love God has prepared for all people.

Now, our enemies do not want you to read the Holy Scripture! They want you to be ignorant of the Word so they can "quote" it to you. Ignorance is your greatest enemy. Those who are not our friends often taunt us, saying "Do you people know what the Bible says about homosexuals?" Yes, I do know what the Bible says and it is all friendly for the lesbian and gay community.

A friend of mine, and a leader in Metropolitan Community Churches, the Rev. Elder Donald Eastman, wrote a pamphlet titled "Homosexuality, Not a Sin, Not a Sickness" in which he wrote about MCC's view of the Bible and homosexuality. Since Don has captured completely my own beliefs concerning these issues, I am going to quote from his writings.

"The Bible is a collection of writings which span more than a thousand years recounting the history of God's relationship with the Hebrew and Christian people. It was written in several languages, embraces many literary forms, and reflects cultures very different from our own. These are important considerations for properly understanding the Bible in its context.

There are vast differences in doctrines between various Christian denominations, all of which use the same Bible. Such differences have led some Christians to claim that other Christians are not really Christians at all! Biblical interpretation and theology differ from church to church.

Biblical interpretation and theology also change from time to time. Approximately 150 years ago in the United States, some Christian teaching held that there was a two-fold moral order: black and white. Whites were thought to be superior to blacks, therefore blacks were to be subservient and slavery was an institution ordained by God.

Clergy who supported such an abhorrent idea claimed the authority of the Bible. The conflict over slavery led to divisions which gave birth to some major Christian denominations. These same denominations, of course, do not support slavery today.

Did the Bible change? No, their interpretation of the Bible did!

New Information Refutes Old Ideas

What influences lead us to new ways of understanding Scripture? New scientific information, social changes, and personal experience are perhaps the greatest forces for change in the way we interpret the Bible and develop our beliefs. Scientific awareness of homosexual orientation did not exist until the nineteenth century.

Most Christian churches, including Metropolitan Community Church, believe the Bible was inspired by God and provides a key source of authority for the Christian faith.

Therefore, what the Bible teaches on any subject, including sexuality, is of great significance. The problem, however, is that sometimes the Bible says very little about some subjects; and popular attitudes about those matters are determined much more by other sources, which are then read into the biblical statements. This has been particularly true of homosexuality. But fortunately, recent scholarship refutes many previous assumptions and conclusions.

GENESIS 19:1-25

What was the sin of Sodom? Some "tele-evangelists" carelessly proclaim that God destroyed the ancient cities of Sodom and Gomorrah because of "homosexuality." Although some theologians have equated the sin of Sodom with homosexuality, a careful look at Scripture corrects such ignorance.

Announcing judgment on these cities in Genesis 18, God sends two angels to Sodom, where Abraham's nephew, Lot, persuades them to stay in his home. Genesis 19 records that "all the people from every quarter" surround Lot's house demanding the release of his visitors so "we might know them." The Hebrew word for "know" in this case, yadha, usually means "have thorough knowledge of." It could also express intent to examine the visitors' credentials, or on rare occasions the term implies sexual intercourse. If the latter was the author's intended meaning, it would have been a clear case of attempted gang rape.

Horrified at this gross violation of ancient hospitality

rules, Lot attempts to protect the visitors by offering his two daughters to the angry crowd, a morally outrageous act by today's standards. The people of Sodom refuse, so the angels render them blind. Lot and his family are then rescued by the angels as the cities are destroyed.

Several observations are important. First, the judgment on these cities for their wickedness had been announced prior to the alleged homosexual incident. Second, all of Sodom's people participated in the assault on Lot's house; in no culture has more than a small minority of the population been homosexual. Third, Lot's offer to release his daughters suggests he knew his neighbors to have heterosexual interests. Fourth, if the issue was sexual, why did God spare Lot, who later commits incest with his daughters? Most importantly, why do all the other passages of Scripture referring to this account fail to raise the issue of homosexuality?

WHAT WAS THE SIN OF SODOM?

Ezekiel 16;48-50 states it clearly: people of Sodom, like many people today, had abundance of material goods. But they failed to meet the needs of the poor and they worshiped idols.

The sins of injustice and idolatry plague every generation. We stand under the same judgment if we create false gods or treat others with injustice.

LEVITICUS 18:22 & 20:13

Christians today do not follow the rules and rituals described in Leviticus. But some ignore its definitions of their own "uncleanness" while quoting Leviticus to condemn "homosexuals." Such abuse of Scripture distorts the Old

Testament meaning and denies a New Testament message.

"You shall not lie with male as one lies with a female; It is an abomination." These words occur solely in the Holiness Code of Leviticus, a ritual manual for Israel's priests. Their meaning can only be fully appreciated in the historical and cultural context of the ancient Hebrew people. Israel, in a unique place as the chosen people of one God, was to avoid the practices of other peoples and gods.

Hebrew religion, characterized by the relation of one God, stood in continuous tension with the religion of the surrounding Canaanites who worshiped the multiple gods of fertility cults. Canaanite idol worship, which featured female and male cult prostitution as noted in Deuteronomy 23:17, repeatedly compromised Israel's loyalty to God. The Hebrew word for a male cult prostitute, qadesh, is mistranslated "sodomite" in some versions of the Bible.

WHAT IS AN "ABOMINATION"?

An abomination is that which God found detestable because it was unclean, disloyal, or unjust. Several Hebrew words were so translated, and the one found in Leviticus, toevah, is usually associated with idolatry, as in Ezekiel, where it occurs numerous times. Given the strong association of toevah with idolatry and the Canaanite religious practice of cult prostitution, the use of toevah regarding male same-sex acts in Leviticus calls into question any conclusion that such condemnation also applies to loving, responsible homosexual relationships.

Rituals and rules found in the Old Testament were given to preserve the distinctive characteristics of the religion and culture of Israel. But, as stated in Galatians 3:22-25, Christians are no longer bound by these Jewish laws. By faith we live in Jesus Christ, not in Leviticus. To be sure, ethical concerns apply to all cultures and peoples in every age. Such concerns were ultimately reflected by Jesus Christ, who said nothing about homosexuality, but a great deal about love, justice, mercy and faith.

ROMANS 1:24-27

Most New Testament books, including the four Gospels, are silent on same-sex acts, and Paul is the only author who makes any reference to the subject. The most negative statement by Paul regarding same-sex acts occurs in Romans 1:24-27 where, in the context of a larger argument on the need of all people for the gospel of Jesus Christ, certain homosexual behavior is given as an example of the "uncleanness" of idolatrous Gentiles.

Does this passage refer to all homosexual acts, or to certain homosexual behavior known to Paul's readers? Romans was written to Jewish and Gentile Christians in Rome, who would have been familiar with the infamous sexual excesses of their contemporaries, especially Roman emperors. They would also have been aware of tensions in the early Church regarding Gentiles and observance of the Jewish laws, as noted in Acts 15 and Paul's letter to the Galatians. Jewish laws in Leviticus mentioned male same-sex acts in the context of idolatry.

WHAT IS "NATURAL"?

Significant to Paul's discussion is the fact that these "unclean" Gentiles exchanged that which was "natural" for them (physin, in the Greek text) for something "unnatural" (para physin). In Romans 11:24, God acts in an "unnatural" way (para physin), to accept the Gentiles. "Unnatural" in these passages does not refer to violation of so-called laws of nature, but rather implies action contradicting one's own nature. In view of this, we should observe that it is "unnatural" (para physin) for a person today with a lesbian or gay sexual orientation to attempt living a heterosexual lifestyle.

Romans 1:26 is the only statement in the entire Bible with a possible reference to lesbian behavior, although the specific intent of this verse is unclear. Some authors have seen in this passage a reference to women adopting a dominant role in heterosexual relationships. Given the repressive cultural expectations placed on women in Paul's time, such a meaning may be possible.

The homosexual practices cited in Romans 1:24-27 were believed to result from idolatry and are associated with some very serious offenses as noted in Romans 1.

Taken in this larger context, it should be obvious that such acts are significantly different from loving, responsible lesbian and gay relationships seen today.

1 Corinthians 6:9 & 1 Timothy 1:10

Any consideration of New Testament statements on same-sex acts must carefully view the social context of the Greco-Roman culture in which Paul ministered. Prostitution and pederasty (sexual relationships of adult men with boys) were the most commonly known male same-sex acts.

In 1 Corinthians 6:9, Paul condemns those who are "effeminate" and "abusers of themselves with mankind," as translated in the King James version. Unfortunately, some newer translations are worse, rendering these words "homosexuals." Recent scholarship unmasks the homophobia behind such mistranslations. The first word – malakos, in the Greek text – which has been translated "effeminate" or "soft," most likely refers to someone who lacks discipline or moral control. The word is used elsewhere in the New Testament but never with reference to sexuality.

The second word, arsenokoitai, occurs once each in 1 Corinthians and 1 Timothy, but nowhere else in other literature of the period. It is derived from two Greek words, one meaning "males" and the other "beds," a euphemism for sexual intercourse. Other Greek works were commonly used to describe homosexual behavior but do not appear here. The larger context of 1 Corinthians 6 shows Paul extremely concerned with prostitution, so it is very possible he was referring to male prostitutes. But many experts now attempting to translate these words have reached a simple conclusion: their precise meaning is uncertain.

No Law Against Love

The rarity with which Paul discusses any form of same-sex behavior and the ambiguity in references attributed to him make it extremely unsound to conclude any such position in the New Testament on homosexuality, especially in the context of loving, responsible relationships.

Since any arguments must be made from silence, it is much more reliable to turn to great principles of the Gospel taught by Jesus Christ and the Apostles.

Love God with all your heart, and love your neighbor as yourself. Do not judge others, lest you be judged. The fruit of the Holy Spirit is love... against such there is no law.

One thing is abundantly clear, as Paul stated in Galatians 5:14: "the whole law is fulfilled in one statement, 'You shall love your neighbor as yourself.'"

Another wonderful friend of mind, Rev. Elder Nancy Wilson, has written a pamphlet entitled, "Our Story Too: Lesbians and Gay Men in the Bible." I want to share with you one part of that pamphlet.

SAME-SEX RELATIONSHIPS IN THE BIBLE

"The stories of two prominent same-sex couples in the Scriptures provide gay men and lesbians with Biblical models of committed love in stressful circumstances.

The book of Ruth is a romantic novel – but not about romance between Ruth and Boaz. Naomi is actually the central character, and Ruth is the "redeemer/hero." Boaz' relationship with Ruth, far from being romantic, is a matter of family duty and property. This story contains the most moving promise of relational fidelity between two persons in all of the Bible: "Entreat me not to leave thee, or to return from following after thee: for whither thou goest, I will go; and where thou lodgest, I will lodge: thy people shall be my people, and thy God my God." (Ruth 1:16)

Although used in heterosexual marriage ceremonies for years, this is a vow between two woman! When their husbands die in battle, Ruth makes this vow to Naomi, her mother-in-law. Ruth marries Boaz, a close relative, and redeems Naomi's place in her own family, also bearing a child for Naomi. Did Ruth and Naomi have a lesbian relationship? There's no way to know, but it is clear the two women had a lifelong, passionate, committed relationship celebrated in Scripture.

UNITED IN A COVENANT OF LOVE

Another story, that of David and Jonathan, occurs in a time when male warrior/lovers were common and considered noble. This tragic triangle of passion, jealousy and political intrigue between Saul, Jonathan and David, leads to one of the most direct expressions of same-sex love in the Bible: "I am distressed for you, my brother Jonathan; you have been very pleasant to me. Your love to me was more wonderful than the love of women." (II Samuel 1:26)

The author is clearly attuned to David's classic male beauty (1 Samuel 16:12) in this story of love and loyalty marked by romance (1 Samuel 18:1-5), secret meetings (1 Samuel 20:1-23; 35-42), kissing and weeping (1 Samuel 20:41), refusal to eat (1 Samuel 28:32-34), and the explicit warrior/lover covenant which David keeps after Jonathan's death (1 Samuel 20:12-17; 42). One cannot read this account without discerning that Jonathan was the love of David's life. Centuries of homophobic Biblical interpretations have kept them in the closet too long!"

Jesus said, "...the truth will set you free." Always remember, the Bible is your friend – no matter what anybody says.

I want to add one more thing about what the Bible says...and does not say about homosexuality. Hear me one more time.

History and the Bible tells us that the pagan religions that surrounded and contaminated Israel's history frequently practiced some form of cult prostitution. Usually it centered on the theme of fertility. Should a wife want to bear children, or a farmer want larger crops or greater flocks, they appealed to the fertility gods. They could engage in sex with the male or female prostitutes available at the temple. I know how bizarre this may sound, but the practice was common. It endured into New Testament times and was frequently assimilated into the worship of Jehovah.

Early in their history, the Jews encountered religious prostitutes [Numbers 25:1-8].

Because of the religion of the Canaanites who lived among them, the religion persisted and repeatedly infiltrated the Jews' religious life. They were continuously plagued by cult prostitution in their own religion even though the law strictly prohibited it [Deuteronomy 23:17-18].

The Bible tells that during the time of the judges, the Jews adopted many of the cruel, immoral practices of the fertility cults [Judges 8-33]. Eventually half the tribe of Manasseh accepted the religion of cult prostitution [I Chronicles 5:25]. Under King Rehoboam there were male prostitutes associated with the hill shrines [1 Kings 14:23-24]. King Ahab fell into Baal worship which included prostitution [2 Chronicles 33:3].

Not everyone participated in the pagan worship, but everyone would have been aware of its presence [1 Kings 15:12; 22:46; 2 Kings 23:7; Ezekiel 16:5-58]. These practices remained common in the world well through the time of Christ and Paul.

When Paul wrote to the church at Corinth, there were 1,000 prostitutes at the temple of the goddess Aphrodite on the Acro-Corinthus.

The writers in the Bible were concerned only with homosexuality as it related to temple prostitutes, because that was their primary contact with the practice. Paul's condemnation [Romans 1;23-27; 1 Corinthians 6:9; 1 Timothy 1:9-10] was the same.

Please hear me one last time, we who are members of a Metropolitan Community Church believe as our Statement of Faith proclaims; "the Bible is the divinely inspired Word of God, showing forth God to every person through the law and the prophets, and finally, completely and ultimately on earth in the being of Jesus Christ." I believe the Bible is the Word of God and is divinely inspired, however, I believe salvation comes only though the sacrifice of Jesus. I believe I am saved by the Blood, not the Book.

CHAPTER FIVE
GOD LOVES LITTLE CHILDREN, ESPECIALLY THE ONE THAT LIVES IN YOU!

Many are the times I have told congregations, "You all have a little boy or a little girl living inside you. And some of you have both!" That comment always makes people laugh. But I also believe it's the truth.

Jesus loved children. At one point in his ministry, his disciples rebuked some parents who wanted Jesus to lay hands on a group of children and pray for them. When Jesus saw what was happening, he called for the children and said, "Permit the little children to come unto me, and forbid them not: for such is the dominion of heaven."

At another time Jesus was asked, "Who is the greatest in the dominion of heaven?" [Matthew 19:14] Jesus placed a child in the midst of them and said, "Truly, I say to you, unless you turn and become like children, you will never enter the dominion of heaven."

And Jesus also said, "Whoever humbles themselves like this child, they will be the greatest in the dominion of heaven." [Matthew 18:1]

I believe with all my heart that God calls all of us to be childlike. Not childish...but childlike.

To keep the child alive inside each of us is a full time job! Have you ever had anyone tell you, "Why don't you act your age?" My answer has always been, "I'm not going to act anything." Being childlike, for me, means allowing the little boy that lives in me out to play once in a while. Thank God that we who are members of the lesbian and gay community can give ourselves permission to be playful. One of the great joys we give to ourselves and to others is the ability to not let others take our joy from us. Because many of us in our community give ourselves permission to be child-like, I believe we can stay forever young.

Over the years, I have learned to be childlike by remembering my own childhood and, now that I am an adult, by learning from the actions of children. I want to share with you several attributes found in most children, attributes that hold powerful lessons for us.

"Uncle Troy, are you ever going to marry?" my five-year-old niece Tiffany asked me as I sat with her nine-year-old brother and ten-year-old sister and my lover in a restaurant on Christmas day.

My lover and I had driven my mother to Las Vegas, Nevada, so she could spend Christmas with my brother, Eugene, and his family. I dearly love my four younger brothers and their families, so whenever I can find the time to be with them I take it. I came out as a gay male to my family over thirty years ago and that never made a difference to my brothers. I had also made up my mind that I would always be open about who I am with my own two sons, as well as to all my nephews and nieces. You should never lie to children.

Now here was my little niece, Tiffany, asking me about marriage.

"Well," I answered her as natural as I could, "Uncle Greg and I have been talking about having a Holy Union," as I looked at him and smiled.

Tiffany looked at us and asked the next logical question. "Well, can you have children?"

"Well, Tiffany, Uncle Greg and I can adopt children," I answered. In my head I thought, "Now is the time to educate Tiffany, Nikki and Lance about my homosexuality."

"You kids do understand that Uncle Greg and I are gay, don't you?" I asked.

"So?" said the two oldest kids at the same time.

"I've seen you on TV, Uncle Troy," my oldest niece said, all smiles.

Greg and I drove the kids back to my brother's home. We said good-bye to my family and drove back to Los Angeles where we lived.

Later, my mother related to me that as soon as Greg and I left, Tiffany marched into the living room where all the adults were assembled and announced, "Uncle Troy and Uncle Greg are going to get married and have a baby. Would you like for it to be a little boy or a little girl?"

According to my mother, the entire family looked at Tiffany to make sure they had heard her correctly. Before anyone could say anything, Tiffany, now knowing she had everyone's attention, said, "Well, I mean, they can adopt a baby. What do you want it to be, a boy or a girl?"

When my mother related the story to me, I laughed and laughed. But I also learned several things about being childlike that day.

First, never lose the gift of asking questions. I was raised in a church that did not encourage its members to question the denomination's rules for being a Christian. I now know I can never again be part of any group that refuses to let me ask questions and find honest answers that work for me, even if they don't for other. I have told the MCC General Conference that we must always be open to a move of the Holy Spirit. We must always be willing to question, even if the answer we receive is, "That's a dumb question."

For the most part, children ask honest questions; kids don't stop to think if the question is going to be embarrassing to anyone, they just ask.

If we are going to be childlike, God requires that we ask questions with the same curiosity that Tiffany did. She asked from the depths of her heart. And here's a lesson from human nature: Even if the question turns out to be embarrassing, the person to whom you posed the question will instinctively know you did not intend it to be so.

Second, never lose the gift of looking for and expecting to find the truth. Children know when we lie to them. (Adults do some of the time.) Children do not have the history of experience to tell them that not every human being is truthful. They believe they will hear the truth when they ask for it. They trust almost everyone around them. Adults who would be childlike must recapture the childlike faith of our childhood.

Third, never lose the gifts of fantasy and imagination. Years ago, I had a friend who frequently said, "I wish I could take a trip and just get out of town for a while."

I would always tell him, "Pack your bags."

You see, I believe what the Christian Scriptures say,

"Faith is the substance of things hoped for, the evidence of things not seen." The gifts of fantasy, faith, and imagination help keep the child within alive and healthy.

So, do the unexpected once in a while.

Years ago, my spouse, Greg Cutts, and I would occasionally put on our leather clothes, drive to North Hollywood, and go dancing at a heterosexual club. Now this was a fascinating thing to watch. When we would go onto the dance floor and start dancing, people would move away from us. I am sure, because of our dress, they thought we were members of the Hells Angels and there to start a fight. All at once he and I would pull out our beautiful black leather fans Greg had made for us and fan dance across the floor.

Everyone smiled, some applauded, and all of us had a great time that night because we let our inner child out to play.

The child in us expects to live as long as we do.

Even in old age, our child wants us to remember that there are things such as touching that are still needed.

God,
My hands are old,
I've never said that out loud before.
But they are.
I was so proud of them once.
They were soft.
Like velvet smoothness of a firm ripe peach.
Now the softness is like worn-out sheets.
Or withered leaves.
When did these slender, graceful hands

Become gnarled, shrunken?
They lie here in my lap;
Naked reminders of the rest of this old body
That has served me too well.

How long has it been since someone touched me?
Twenty years?
Twenty years I've been a widow.
Respected.
Smiled at.
But never touched.
Never held close to another body.
Never held so close and warm that loneliness was
Blotted out.

I remember how my mother used to hold me, God.
When I was hurt in spirit or flesh
She would gather me close
Stroke my silky hair and caress
My back with her warm hands.
Oh, God, I'm so lonely!

I remember the first boy who ever kissed me.
We were both so new at that.
the taste of young lips and popcorn,
The feeling deep inside of mysteries to come.
I remember Hank and the babies.

How can I remember them but together?
Out of the fumbling, awkward attempts of new lovers
Came the babies.
And as they grew, so did our love.
And, God, Hank didn't seem to care if my body thickened
And faded a little.
He still loved it,
And touched it.

And we didn't mind if we were no longer "beautiful."
And the children hugged me a lot.
Oh, God, I'm lonely!

Why didn't we raise the kids to be silly and affectionate?
As well as dignified and proper?
You see, they do their duty.
They drive up in their fine cars.
They come to my room and pay their respects.
They chatter brightly
And reminisce.

But they don't touch me.
They call me "Mom" or "Grandma"
Never Minnie.
My mother called me Minnie.
And my friends.
Hank called me Minnie, too.
But they're gone.
And so is Minnie.
Only Grandma is here.
And, God! She is lonely!

[from Images; Women in Transition by Donna Swanson. The Upper Room: Nashville, Tenn.]

In one way or another, "Minnie" lives in all of us, remembering, being the child.

CHAPTER 6
ALWAYS LISTEN TO THE VOICE OF GOD.

God still talks to human beings. You can carry on a conversation with the Divine. I know. Because I do. I realize that a lot of people have problems with believing that God still talks to humans, but I can assure you that God does.

One of my favorite comedians is Lily Tomlin. I am told she once said, "When we talk to God, it's called prayer. When God talks to us, it's called schizophrenia." I have a feeling that describes what many people believe about hearing the voice of God in the 21st Century.

There are many people in the Bible who listen to the voice of God. One of my favorite Biblical characters whom I learned about in Sunday School was Noah.

When I was a young boy, my family attended a small Baptist church in Central Florida. Across the street from our church was a bar. Every Sunday when I left Sunday School, I would see the sign for the bar. The name of the bar was "Noah's Ark." Their slogan was, "come on in children, it's going to rain!" I would laugh out loud every time I saw it.

In case you haven't heard of the story of Noah, let me tell it to you in my own words, as if the story was happening today. Then you can read the Bible story yourself as found in the Book of Genesis [6:9-7:6].

One day as Noah was working, God spoke to him and said, "Noah, I am going to destroy all life on earth. And I'm going to do it with water. I want you to build a boat, an ark, in which I will save your household and some creatures I will send to you."

Because Noah was a person of spiritual faith and because God had spoken to him, Noah immediately started to build the Ark.

It wasn't long before someone saw Noah working and stopped by to ask him, "Noah, what are you building?"

"God told me to build a boat, because there is going to be a flood. The boat will save my family and some animals which God is going to send me," said Noah.

The person laughed and laughed.

"God couldn't have spoken to you. that's crazy. In case you haven't noticed, there are no rivers around here. No lakes, no pools, not even any creeks. We're not close to any oceans, and if you haven't noticed, we don't even get dew around here! See, God couldn't have spoken to you."

How did Noah respond?

Why, he just kept building the Ark.

And the people kept laughing.

I'm sure that one day Ms. Noah came home and said to her husband, "Honey, I can't even visit with the other women of the village. They all think you have lost your mind and are making fun of all our family. Can't you rethink what you are doing?"

But Noah just kept building his Ark.

I am sure there must have been two gay males who walked by Noah's house and saw Noah building the Ark.

I can imagine one putting his hand on his hip and saying, "Girlfriend, look at Miss Noah! He's building himself a boat!"

Everybody kept laughing until the day it started to rain. Noah had listened to the voice of God.

Another individual in the Bible who listened to the voice of God was a remarkable woman named Deborah. Deborah stands out as one of the wisest of all the women named in the Hebrew Scriptures. She is one of several females in Scripture distinguished as being endowed with the prophetic gift, which means the ability to discern the mind and purpose of God and declare it to others. She was the medium between God and God's people.

Deborah was the fifth "Judge" or ruler of Israel raised up by God to deliver God's people from bondage. As the position of women in those days was of a distinctly subordinate character, Deborah's prominence as a ruler is remarkable. All Israel was under her jurisdiction and the Bible says that she dispensed righteousness, justice and mercy to the people.

There was one problem. Israel had lost much of its freedom to a group of people known as the Canaanites.

One day God spoke to Deborah and told her how to overthrow the Canaanite army that was oppressing Israel.

She listened to the voice of God and then went to the general of her army, Barak. She told him what God had said. Long years of slavery and repeated failures made Barak hesitate. Ultimately, he decided to lead the army and insisted Deborah go with him. I am sure he must have thought that only she knew if God had really spoken to her. But he had the faith to believe her because she was willing to participate in the battle.

What a battle! With only 10,000 warriors in their army, they came against an army of 100,000 fighters, and some 900 iron chariots. When combat came, the dauntless spirit of Deborah did not waiver. From a human standpoint, the odds were against her. But she looked above and beyond the circumstances. She knew God was her ally and she knew a divine truth: "If God be for us, who can stand against us." She and Israel won the battle that day!

After the victory over the Canaanites, she ruled with equity over a land that could now rest from 40 years of war and captivity because she listened to the voice of God. You can read the entire story in the Bible in the Book of Judges [Chapters 4 and 5].

One last person whose story is found in the Bible is also one of my favorites. that's the prophet Moses. According to the biblical story, God spoke to Moses. God called Moses to lead the Children of Israel out of slavery in Egypt to the Promised Land.

What a job! The Children of Israel were not the easiest people to lead. Moses learned very quickly they were either on the mountain top or down in the valley. There was no in between for them. In our day and age a psychiatrist would probably diagnose them collectively as manic depressives.

So Moses' job was not easy. The Children of Israel were forever accusing Moses of leading them out in the desert to die. At one point they were even willing to go back into slavery because there, they told Moses, they at least had "cucumbers and garlic."

Can you imagine being willing to go back into slavery for kosher pickles? that's what they were talking about. Before you laugh, think about what we who are members of the homosexual community have been willing to sell ourselves for. Many of us are still in denial about who we are. We are slaves to heterocomformity.

Many were the times when the Children of Israel needed food and water during their journey. And many were the times Moses went to God in prayer for those needs. In almost every circumstance when Moses prayed for water, God told him to take his staff and hit a rock. And when he did, water would gush forth from the rock.

One day after leading the Children of Israel for almost forty years and listening to them grumble and complain about his leadership, Moses found that they needed water again. As always Moses went to God in prayer.

This time God told Moses to walk up to a rock and talk to it [Numbers 20:1-13]. I am sure I know how Moses must have felt. He was angry. He probably thought, "What's the use? These ungrateful people just don't care about me or any other leader." I'm also sure he must have thought, "No matter what God says, if I start talking to rocks these people will believe I've lost my mind."

And so Moses did what he had always done. He took his staff and hit the rock, just as he had done before. And sure enough water flowed from it. But God was not amused!

"Moses," God said. "I told you to talk to the rock, not hit it. I was trying to teach the Children of Israel a new lesson."

God told Moses that he had sinned. That is, Moses had not done what God had told him to do. God knows, the seven last words of the Christian Church are, "We've never done it this way before."

When I have preached on this story from the Bible, I always tell the audience that if God speaks to anyone in the church and tells them to talk to the walls, just go do it!

I tell them, "You don't know who's on the other side of that wall waiting for the message you have to deliver."

People often ask me, "Rev. Perry how does God speak to you?"

In all my years of ministry, I have learned that God uses many ways to speak to us. God has spoken to me in an audible voice four times in my life. God has spoken to me "in my gut" and through other people thousands of times. Here is the secret: God will speak to us if we will only start a conversation with God.

That conversation is called prayer. "People ought always to pray," the Bible tells us. There is a familiar expression that says we learn by doing." Prayer presents no exception to this rule.

As a Christian, I pray in the name of Jesus. In the record of Christ's last discourse in the Upper Room as preserved for us in the Book of John, Jesus repeatedly told his disciples that in praying they are always to ask in His name, and that by thus asking they will receive. "Whatsoever you ask in my name, that will I do." [John 14: 13] "If you ask anything in my name, I will do it." [14:14] "That whatsoever you ask of the divine Parent in my name, God may give you" [15:16]. "Until now you have asked nothing in my name; ask and you shall receive" [16:24]. "At that day you shall ask in my name" [16:26].

Listen to God with the ears of faith when things go wrong. Many are the times God has spoken to me and I almost missed the message because I wasn't listening with my ears of faith. I have had to learn to stop doing all the talking during prayer time so God could talk to me.

That "stop doing all the talking" is what I call "meditation time." It's the quiet time when I hear that "still small voice" deep within myself.

Let me illustrate how this works.

In July, 1974 I received an invitation from gay activists in Australia to visit and speak as a part of their multi-city "Campaign Against Moral Persecution." Reverend Lee Carlton, who was at that time my assistant pastor in the Mother Church, and his partner, Christian, joined me on the journey. Unfortunately, our adventure Down Under was unexpectedly marred from the outset.

We had arrived in Brisbane, Queensland, and had been met by a young officer of the Salvation Army. He introduced us to other lesbian and gay Christians and we conducted a worship service for the small group. The last day we were there, John, the Salvation Army officer called us with some bad news.

"Pastor, I'm sorry to have to tell you this, but I have received a telephone call from the office of the Campaign Against Moral Persecution in Sydney. They said they didn't want you to come and they will not sponsor the rest of your trip in Australia."

To put it mildly, we were shocked. John went on to explain that the non-religious in C.A.M.P. had decided, on political grounds, that they would not receive us.

So Lee, Christian, and I met in my hotel room to discuss what we should do. We all agreed that we felt God had led us to Australia. We believed we were not only to speak to political groups, but we were also to use the trip to start Metropolitan Community Churches there. We went to God in prayer.

What should we do? We all agreed that we believed God had opened the doors for us to be there. However, we didn't know anyone in Sydney. Not a single soul. So we prayed again.

"Troy," Lee said, "I believe God wants us to go on to Sydney, whether anybody wants us there or not."

I agreed. "I believe God wants us to go. When we get to Sydney, we'll print leaflets and invite people to a worship service at the hotel where we are staying. We'll go to the gay bars and pass them out."

"Well," Christian said, "okay. Lets do it."

One hour after we had made our decision to go, the phone in my hotel room rang. It was John.

"I can't believe what just happened," he said. "I just got off the phone with the president of Acceptance, a new, small gay Catholic group in Sydney. They just received word that you three are here in Australia. They want you to come on to Sydney and they want to sponsor your visit there."

It was with much relief and anticipation that we arrived in Sydney.

We were met by representatives from every television

station, radio network, and newspaper syndicate with offices in Sydney.

From that moment on, wherever we went in any part of Australia, neither Lee nor I could move, say, or do anything without rapt media attention. If a carnival atmosphere was created, we participated willingly, and in the end we won all of the games. During the month we remained in Australia, I appeared on forty-eight television and twenty-two radio shows. Every paper and magazine in the country ran daily articles about us. Wherever we went, groups formed and began thinking about spirituality and sexual freedom in ways they had never considered before.

We simply asked the question, "Are you interested in becoming a part of MCC?" And congregations began to form with a nucleus of interested people. That step enabled Metropolitan Community Church to become important in the future of Australia, because once we had offered the suggestion, Australians set out on their own to keep the dream alive.

I believe all of this happened because Lee, Christian, and I listened to the voice of God with the ears of faith. After prayer we believed we should go. We believed that was God's will for us. And I believe because we were faithful, God was faithful to us and opened Australia's door to us.

I have to share with you, however, that God knew our plan to pass out literature in front of gay bars would have been a poor solution to our dilemma. As we quickly discovered, gay bars such as we have in America did not exist in Australia at that time. But God knew our hearts and knew we wanted to be faithful to God's work. And God gave us the Australian media instead of having us pass out leaflets.

Always, always, always listen to the voice of God in your life. In 1987, I received a letter from the National Conference of Catholic Bishops. It stated, in essence, "Dear Rev. Perry, the National Conference of Catholic Bishops would like to invite you and another representative of the Universal Fellowship of Metropolitan Community Churches to participate in an ecumenical service in Columbia, South Carolina, where His Holiness, Pope John Paul II, will officiate." I read the letter through several times. Why would the Catholic Bishops in the U. S. be inviting me to be a part of the Pope's visit when the Pope had just instructed the Bishops to not permit Dignity, the lesbian and gay Catholic organization to use church property for their Mass? The Pope had banned priests from conducting the Mass at those services.

My first reaction was this must be a joke. My second thought was, "I bet some gay person working in the Bishops' office said, 'Oh, let's just add Rev. Perry's name to the guest list.'"

I recalled a time in the early 1970's when my other half wanted me to accompany him to the small Catholic Church in our neighborhood. His grandmother had just died. I agreed. I certainly have no objections to worshiping with another denomination. We attended the seven o'clock Mass. All went well until communion was served. Everyone in the congregation had received the sacrament at the altar except me. When I arrived and knelt, a wrathful priest unexpectedly turned on me.

"You're not Catholic!" he said in such a way as to instantly put me on the defensive.

"No, sir," I replied, "but I've received communion in a Catholic Church before."

"You are not going to receive it here!" the priest snapped. "I've seen you on television. I know who you are!"

"Well, Father," I tried to reason, "can't we Christians eat at the same table with each other? After all, I have received communion in the Catholic Church before."

Very slowly the priest said, "That may be true, but you will not receive here."

Anger dimmed my vision and I wanted to lash back. All I could think about were the words of Jesus in the Book of Matthew, "And whosoever shall not receive you, nor hear your words, when you depart out of that house or city, shake off the dust of your feet."

I thought as I turned to leave, "That's what I will do. I'll shake the dust off my feet against the Catholic Church."

Then the spirit of reason took over and said to me, "You have to do better than that."

When I reached the front door of the church I paused long enough to lay both of my hands on the sides of the door and I fervently prayed, "Lord, let me be the last gay person to walk through the portals of this church who has to put up with this kind of humiliation."

And here I was just a few years later holding an invitation to be a part of the Pope's visit.

I can only suppose our invitation had something to do with Metropolitan Community Church's continuing ecumenical dialogue with the National Council of Churches. But whatever the reason, I decided to attend. And, since the invitation was for me and another guest, I asked the Reverend Nancy Wilson to accompany me. I believed it was important for my Catholic sisters and brothers to see a woman in the collar. I know God doesn't look at our gender when God calls us to be clergy. The Christian Scriptures tell us that in Jesus there is no difference in males and females [Galatians 3:28].

Because we were guests of the Catholics and had accepted their invitation, there was little we felt we could do to address the problems Catholic homosexuals were having other than to give witness to the fact that we, a lesbian and gay man, existed as living proof that homosexuals continue to be a great part of God's ecumenical celebration. With this as our intention, Nancy and I each wore buttons that read: "GOD IS GREATER THAN AIDS – Metropolitan Community Churches."

Our buttons attracted attention because, among the four hundred invited clergy in attendance, we were the only people at the service wearing anything unusual. Ministers approached us to read the message pinned on our robes. Their reactions ranged all the way from "We're glad M.C.C. is here," spoken with warmth to inquiries followed by exclamations like "God is greater than – AIDS??!!!"

Some of the clergy expressed shock that we (even as they) had been invited to be a part of the Catholics' large-scale public event. "Doesn't the Roman Church know who they are?" we heard airy preachers ask.

"Evidently they do," Nancy replied.

We marched into the stadium which held 75,000 spectators for the service.

Months later I was having dinner in a restaurant in Los Angeles, when a man approached my table and said, "Reverend Perry, I was in South Carolina and saw you at the service. A friend of mind pointed you out to me. I pastor a Roman Catholic Church here in town."

"Well, I am glad to meet you," I said. "Which Catholic church do you pastor?"

He told me. It was the church where I had been denied communion years before. I quit smiling and said a very unpleasant, "Oh." He didn't notice my body language change.

"I just wanted to tell you that I have started a ministry to lesbian and gay persons in our church," he said. "I want everybody to feel welcome to our Mass."

"Hallelujah!" I almost shouted.

"Pardon?" he asked, confused.

"Hallelujah!" I said again.

I then told him my story of what had happened to me in the church he was now pastoring and what I had prayed for back then. When I finished he said, "Hallelujah!"

Always listen to the voice of God when you need healing.

Let me tell you about Rev. Steve Pieters. I helped plan his funeral.

I first met Steve's parents in Los Angeles, at a dinner honoring Steve's work in helping other persons with AIDS. We knew the doctors said Steve would not live beyond

1984. He had been diagnosed with two kinds of cancer: lymphoma and Kaposi's Sarcoma.

And then something miraculous happened to Steve.

You see, in 1994 Steve was invited, along with 13 other leaders of AIDS/HIV religious organizations, to the White House by President Bill Clinton. Steve was then director of our denomination's AIDS Ministry. Steve was invited to a breakfast meeting with the President and Vice President Al Gore.

Steve was placed at the table next to Mr. Clinton and across from the Vice President. The President talked to Steve throughout breakfast. Steve told the President his story of his fight with AIDS/HIV and how he had almost died eleven years before. The President asked, "Steve, what do you attribute to the fact that you have had two kinds of cancer go into remission and are one of the longest survivors of AIDS in America?"

"Well," Steve said, "my doctors believe that the experimental drug Suramin, which everyone else in my control group died from, somehow helped me."

"But what do you believe?" the President asked.

"I believe that God touched my body and gave me healing," Steve answered.

We who are part of Metropolitan Community Churches believe in healing that comes to us by way of doctors and drugs. We also believe in healing that takes place even when the doctors have given up. We believe God is greater that any disease and it is God's will that we live in wholeness.

Disease is not God's gift to human beings. There is not

one statement in the Christian Scriptures that tell us God wishes humans to suffer from sickness.

A preacher once told me that AIDS was God's gift to gay people. I do not believe that AIDS is God's gift to gay people anymore than I believe that sickle cell anemia is God's gift to Black people, or toxic shock syndrome is God's gift to women, or Legionnaire's Disease is God's gift to members of the American Legion for being too patriotic! I do not believe in a theology of the common cold! I do not for one second believe in a type of God who passes out diseases. What an awful, erratic God that would be! Nowhere in Scripture did Jesus once say, "If you don't straighten up and fly right, God's going to give you a disease." Read the Bible for yourself! Disease is exactly and only that – disease.

Christian Scripture relates this story: "As he went on his way Jesus saw a man who had been blind from birth. His disciples asked him, 'Rabbi, why was this man born blind? Who sinned, this man or his parents?' 'It is not that he or his parents sinned,' Jesus answered. He was born blind so that God's power might be displayed in curing him" [John 9:1-3].

God is the Great Healer. One of the first things God told Moses about God was, "I am your Sovereign who heals you" [Exodus 15:26]. The psalmist David knew this as a divine truth and sang, "Bless God, O my soul, and all that is within me, bless God's holy name. Bless God, O my soul, and do not forget all God's benefits – who forgives all your iniquity, who heals all your diseases [Psalms 103:1-3].

We who are part of the Christian faith believe that Jesus, the Christ, was God-in-the-flesh who came and lived among us. Jesus was not only savior, but healer as well. I believe a prophet in the Hebrew Scriptures foretold the coming of the Christ when he said, "Who could have believed what we have heard?

To whom has the power of Yahweh been revealed? He grew up before Yahweh like a young plant whose roots are in parched ground; he had no beauty, no majesty to catch our eyes, no grace to attract us to him. He was despised, shunned by all, a man of suffering and acquainted with infirmity; one of those from whom people hide their faces, spurned, and we held him in no esteem. Surely he has borne our infirmities and carried our diseases; yet we accounted him stricken, struck down by God, and afflicted. But he was wounded for our transgressions, crushed for our iniquities; upon him was the punishment that made us whole, and by his stripes we are healed" [Isaiah 53:1-5].

The Christian Scriptures tell us that Jesus used this verse from the Hebrew Scripture [Isaiah 61:1-2] when he preached his first sermon: "The spirit of God is on me, for God has anointed me to bring good news to the afflicted. God has sent me to proclaim liberty to captives, sight to the blind, to let the oppressed go free, and to proclaim a year acceptable to God" [Luke 4:18]. After preaching that first sermon Jesus began his ministry to people. If the sick were brought to Jesus, if the sick touched Jesus, they were healed. If friends or loved ones asked Jesus to heal sick people who could not come to Jesus, Jesus healed them. And I believe Jesus is still healing today.

Listen to the voice of God when religion gets in the way of healing! Religious people had a bad habit of attacking Jesus almost every time he healed the sick [Matthew 9:1-8; 32-34; 12:9-12; 22-32, Mark 2:3-12; 3:1-6; 22-30, Luke 5:17-25; 6:1-11; 11:14-26; 13:10-17; 14:1-6, John 5:1-18; 9:1-34].

Remember, the only people that Jesus ever said were going to hell are religious hypocrites [Matthew 23:15,33; Mark 9:42-48; 2 Peter 2:1-4]. Know that it is God's desire that you be well in mind, body, and soul no matter what other people – even well meaning people – think.

The act of death is the time of healing for many of us.

My mother was told by her doctor that she had breast cancer. My mother handled the news as well as one can. I didn't handle it well at all. I tried to do what any good child would do if given that news: I cried, I prayed, I always tried to give my mother hope that she could somehow beat the cancer. And for four years she did.

During those four years we had highs and lows. At times the cancer would be in remission; other times we knew it was not. The cancer was not my mother's only health problem. Five years before she was diagnosed with cancer, she had been diagnosed with diabetes. That was even harder to handle than the cancer. Mother loved sweets.

My partner, Phillip, and I taught ourselves how to give Mother her injections of insulin. She would be so good, as we called it, for a week or two, and then she would have to have her sweets. Sometimes I would hear Mom in the middle of the night in the kitchen. When I went to the kitchen the next morning, I would discover that Mom had eaten half of a pie or a cake.

Because she was my mother and because I always knew that getting into an argument would not work, I would always say, "Mom, won't all that sugar hurt you?" Usually Mom would ignore me, but sometimes she would laughingly say, "Just give me more insulin. I wanted that cake."

Mother loved it when I travelled. That's when she and Phillip were home alone for the weekend. Phillip would always ask Mother, "Why don't you and I go out and get something to eat? Where would you like to go?"

Phillip knew Mom would always pick the one place I wouldn't take her.

"Oh," Mother would answer, "let's go to the IHOP [the International House of Pancakes]."

And away they went whether I liked it or not!

The day arrived when the doctor told Mother the words none of us ever wanted to hear: "Mrs. Perry, there isn't anything else we can do. I am taking you off all medication."

My mother told the doctor she understood.

"Is there anything you would like to eat? You can have anything," said the doctor.

To break the tension I said, "How about a piece of cake?"

With a smile in her eyes she shot back, "And a piece of pie too." And then she shook her head and said, "No, I really don't want anything."

The doctor laughed, knowing of my and Mother's fights over the years about her diabetes.

He became serious again and said, "We will make you as comfortable as possible."

Mother went into a coma the next day. Three days later she died.

How I missed my Mom. She had come to live with me six months after I had founded the Metropolitan Community Church in Los Angeles. She lived with me for 20 years.

Not only was she my Mother, she was my best friend and confidante. To say that I missed my mother would be an understatement.

For three months after Mother's death I felt so alone. Phillip would notice my loneliness and say, "I miss Mom, too."

One night I went to sleep and dreamed that I was in a beautiful room. I dreamed my mother was standing with me. Mother was standing by a low marble table. She was dressed to the "10's" as I called it when I thought she looked perfect. On the table was a crystal bowl and in the bowl were gumdrops. Mother reached over and picked up two or three pieces of candy and started to eat them. I said, as I always did when I saw my mother eat sweets, "Mother, won't that hurt you?"

My mother looked at me, smiled, and said with wonder in her voice, "Troy, I don't have diabetes anymore!"

Listen to the voice of God when you look death in the face. The Children of Israel did and lived. The story is told in the Hebrew Scriptures [Numbers 21: 6-7]. The Children of Israel believed they sinned against Moses and God because they camped in a place that was inhabited by serpents. Many people were bitten by the snakes and started dying. The Scriptures tell us that the people asked forgiveness for their sins. They asked Moses to pray that the snakes would be taken away from them and to pray for healing for those who were bitten. Moses prayed and God spoke: "Make a bronze serpent and put it up on a pole; anyone who is bitten can look at it and live" [Numbers 21:8]. So Moses made a bronze snake and put it up on a pole. Then when anyone was bitten by a snake and looked at the bronze snake, they lived.

I believe with all my heart that if you have a terminal illness you have to "look at it and live." You need to live with it and die living. Every second, minute, and hour of a day should be yours to live. We don't have to fear death; it's not the end. The Christian Scriptures tell us, "To be absent from our bodies, is to be present with God." [2 Corinthians 5:7-8].

When God talks, listen!

Seven weeks after I held the first service of Metropolitan Community Church, I received a phone call.

"Is this the Rev. Troy Perry?" the voice asked.

"Yes, it is," I said.

"I wonder if I could meet with you. My name is Rev. Jones [not his real name]."

He went on to tell me he lived in Hollywood and asked if I would come to his house the following night to meet him and his roommate about "your church."

The next night my lover and I arrived at the address given to me. Rev. Jones and his roommate met us at the door of their apartment and invited us in.

After we were seated and given drinks, Rev. Jones got right to the point.

"Why did you start your Church?" he asked.

I shared my testimony with him about my life, my call to ministry, my coming out as a gay male, and my believing that God had called me to start a church as a special outreach to the lesbian and gay community, but with its doors open to all.

When I finished speaking, Rev. Jones just stared at me for the longest time, as though trying to make up his mind about something. Then he said, "It will never work. God does not speak to people the way you described it."

He then launched into a long diatribe about the gay

community and how he had tried to help it and how it didn't want help. "No, your church will never work," he said shaking his head.

"Rev. Jones, it's not my church, its God's," I said.

"Well, it still will not work," he said.

Ten years later while I was shopping, I heard a voice say, "Rev. Perry?" I turned around and it was Rev. Jones.

"I just wanted to tell you I'm sorry for what I said to you years ago. I was wrong, and you and God have proved it."

As I have said, if God has directed you to do something, do it. God is the highest authority we have in our lives. I am sure that had I gone to people and asked for their permission to found Metropolitan Community Church, I would have met lots of Rev. Jones's who would have discouraged me from holding the first service. I believe I would still be waiting to found Metropolitan Community Church if I had listened to people.

After Metropolitan Community Church started I found a book written by Robert W. Wood, titled, Christ and The Homosexual [Vantage Press, Inc., 1960]. The words of Rev. Wood were radical for the time in which they were written and they gave us hope. And yet Rev. Wood's message was that a church group such as M. C. C. could not be successful once it was started.

He wrote:

> "Having recognized the validity of making the ministry of the local church available to those homosexuals who will avail themselves of it, we ask, what type of ministry? "Be specific!" is the cry. A local church need not, indeed should not, go out of its way to minister just to this particular group, any more than to any segment of the population.
>
> "No concentrated publicity is needed beyond the news spread by one or two homosexuals who have found meaningful religious experience in some phase of the parish program. A church certainly never need feel ashamed for ministering to this group, nor need it make apologies to the community. But it does not have to hang "Welcome" banners across the door. This would only drive the boys away. For the fundamental lesson to be learned in ministering to them is that they wish to be loved and treated like anyone else and accepted on equal terms.
>
> "The church program prepared especially for homosexuals will fail because few if any will attend. To do so would be to advertise themselves."

I believe with all my heart that God will be faithful to God's word. God will keep the promises God makes. If we listen after we pray, God will speak to us!

Always listen to the voice of God!

CHAPTER SEVEN
THE MAIN THING IS TO KEEP THE MAIN THING THE MAIN THING

There is one thing you must remember in life: God loved you so much that God gave you "free will." God put you in charge of your life. You are not a robot. You have to make choices in life about you. You decide if you are going to permit God or other human beings into your life after you reach what we Christians call "the age of accountability." That takes place when you reach an age when you understand the difference between right and wrong – when you can "think on your own."

When you are a child, others think for you. At some point in life, you think for yourself. You have reached the age of accountability. You become in charge of a universe existing within you. No one, including God, may enter that universe without your permission. That's what "free will" means. And that's how God wants it. You are in charge!

The day I woke up and discovered I was in charge, it almost freaked me out. When I realized that I had to make choices for me, I wasn't sure I liked that. It was easier when Mother and Dad or others made decisions for me. If the decisions were wrong they took the blame, not me. But I have reached the age of accountability, and for good or bad, I am in charge.

You are in charge of the way you live your life!

Life is all about living. The Bible tells us that God spoke to all of us once and said, "I place before you life and death."

And then God gave us a clue: "Choose life." Living is mostly about attitude. You can have a good life or a bad one – and your attitude makes much of the difference.

For eight years now, as I write this, I have kept a clipping of a small article I found in a magazine. In fact, it is taped to the mirror where I shave each morning. Regrettably, I do not know who the author is. Every morning when I am at home, I see this and I quickly read it: "You are in charge of your life. You are in control of your attitude. It's not your boss, your job, your parents, or the breaks that create your attitude. It's you."

How you think and how you react are totally up to you. Looking for bad things to happen can actually make them happen. People with negative attitudes generally expect such situations as losing a job, bankruptcy, poor employee relations, unpleasant working conditions, and failure. Pessimists expect to feel bad and get sick, so they do. On the other hand, reality-oriented, positive thinking can influence us to overcome significant obstacles. If you really believe a goal can be reached, your attitude releases new energy that will help bring about the achievement of that goal.

During every moment of your life, you program your attitude to work for you or against you. Attitude itself is a neutral mechanism. It's only a means to an end. Whatever your objectives and goals are, their direction is set by your attitudes, whether positive or negative, true or false, right or wrong, self-enhancing or self-destroying. Your attitude creates the outcome according to your instructions, much like a computer whose output is determined by its inputs. Positive images can bolster you even when everything is going wrong. And until you find a solution to the problem, or the situation changes, you've maintained your energy.

You've not caved in. You've survived in the face of an obstacle. Your inner attitude will shine through to your external behavior, catapulting you to ultimate success. We are not responsible for what happens "out there" nor for what others do or think. We are responsible only for how we choose to respond. That's our attitude. The responsibility for us is ours.

As an adult, choosing Life means you do not have to be a victim anymore. I have met members of the lesbian and gay community who have been victimized as children. I also know that all lesbian and gay people have been victimized in general ways by the culture we live in. But we must not continue to live as victims. Our community is filled with stories of people who have learned to live as themselves and have broken free of the victim mold.

Rev. Joseph Gilbert, a friend and colleague of mine, frequently reminds me of this story about a man that both of us knew. Van was probably sixty years old or so. He always dressed in male clothing on the streets of Sacramento, Calif., where he lived, except in summer, when he wore a black nylon waitress' skirt, because, he said, "It keeps me cooler." Metropolitan Community Church had come into Van's life like a burst of light with the message that you can be exactly who you know God to have created you to be! So Van had begun to wear "women's" clothing all the time...and shoes that any ninety year old nun would have loved. Van might not have described the clothing he wore as women's clothing.

One day a child came up to him as he was walking and asked, "Why are you wearing women's shoes?"

"Those aren't women's shoes," Van said, "those are my shoes."

Van, you see, had learned to break free of other people's limited vision and experience and had learned to fully be himself.

A young Marine started attending the local Metropolitan Community Church in Long Beach, Calif. He was the head of the military police for Los Angeles County. Military intelligence followed him to church one day and photographed him going in and coming out of our predominantly gay church.

Two weeks later he was ordered to appear for a hearing with the head of military intelligence. "I have photographs of you going to a queer church," the man said.

"It's not a queer church," the young Marine answered. "It's a Christian church."

"Well, it's a homosexual church," shot back the man.

"No, sir. It's a Christian church. You don't have to be a homosexual to attend that church. It's open to everybody," said the young man.

"Well, I believe where there is smoke there is fire," said the officer. "Are you a homosexual?"

"Sir, I am a good soldier. I do my job. I have won commendation after commendation for my work as a member of the military police. That's all you should concern yourself with," he said. "I am not going to start answering any questions about my sex life. That is none of your business."

"So, are you telling me you are a heterosexual then?" asked the officer with annoyance in this voice.

"No, sir," the Marine answered, "I'm not telling you any

thing about my sex life. As I said, I'm not going to answer questions like that. It's none of your business."

One month later the Marine was ordered to appear before a military judge where he was asked again, "Are you a homosexual?"

Again the answer was, "It's none of your business."

"Are you a heterosexual?"

Again, "Its none of your business."

The judge ordered the Marine to undergo a polygraph test to see if he was lying. On the day of the test, the polygraph operator browbeat the young man with the same questions for over an hour.

"Are you a homosexual?"

"It's none of your business."

"Are you a heterosexual?"

"It's none of your business."

Finally, the officer who had first questioned the young Marine and who was sitting in on the test, leaned over the polygraph operators shoulder and asked, "So, does the test prove he's lying?"

The polygraph operator pushed back from his machine and faced the officer. "No sir," he answered. "It shows he's telling the truth. It's none of your business!"

You are in charge of who you give power to over you. Becoming a non-victim means you recognize that you will never intentionally give power to people or things that diminish your God-given right to make choices.

For over 30 years I have lived as an openly gay man in one of the most homophobic nations on earth. I made up my mind when I "came out" that I would be true to who I believed God created me to be. I believe I was born a homosexual. My homosexuality is a gift from God and I owe no mortal an apology for that gift. As the result of that gift, I chose to live the life that all human beings should expect to live: One of peace, one that sees my honest needs met, and one where I hopefully can give back to others what I believe God has given to me.

I fully expect the community of which I am a part to treat me as any other member of that community; no more, but absolutely no less. I expect to be able to work in any job where I am qualified.

In the more than thirty years I have lived by my creed, I stopped being a victim. I learned a divine truth: It's easier to get forgiveness than it is to get permission.

The first conscious decision I made when I "came out" was that I would never again lie about my sexual orientation. That means that if I am asked I have really three honest answers. The first is, "Yes." The second is, "Why do you ask that question?" And the third is, "It's none of your business."

The second decision I made was I would be natural in the way I carried myself. I would be the same person in public that I am in private. For example, when my spouse Phillip meets me at the airport after I have been away from home, we kiss because we have missed each other.

Now, in my experience, two men kissing in an airport does get noticed by about one percent of those present. I believe those people think one of three things. The first is, "Well, isn't that sweet, two brothers." The second is, "Well, isn't that sweet, a dad and his son." And the third is, "I don't care what I think I saw. That couldn't have happened."

I have yet to have anyone say anything to me because they saw my spouse and I show natural affection to each other in an airport.

I do remember however my spouse and I walking down the street in our neighborhood one day. We were going to visit some friends and we were holding hands. Suddenly, I heard someone shouting from a passing automobile.

"Queers!" he yelled.

Now, I'm not shy by nature. So I shouted back, "Get used to it!"

I guess people think they are brave when they are in an automobile going sixty miles an hour.

I was the first openly gay male appointed to a county commission in American history. I was appointed to the Los Angeles County Commission on Human Relations, whose work is to make recommendations to the county government. It works to insure all of our citizens are treated with equality and are not discriminated against.

I wish I could I tell you that I was welcomed with open arms by the other commissioners, but that was not the case. The day I was sworn in, half of the commission members were not present. I was told that they had problems with my homosexuality. And these were people who lesbians and gay males had been expecting to make recommendations for them to our government. For the first six months, I made sure all those commissioners got to know me – not as a label, but as a person. And once I believed they thought I had more in common with them than I had differences, I held up my hand to be recognized in our meeting. I made the motion that "sexual orientation" be placed in the non-discrimination clauses of Los Angeles County. My motion was quickly seconded, it passed, and as they say, the rest is history.

Which brings me to the third decision I made then. I decided I would do everything in my power to educate everyone I came in contact with about my sexual orientation and the lesbian and gay community of which I am a member.

The most important work that the lesbian and gay Nation world-wide can do is the job of educating the larger culture about who we are. To know us is to love us. We have more in common with our neighbors than they think or are often willing to admit.

The "radical right" in cultures all over the world is using the Big Lie to define who we are. We must not let that happen. They are trying to pass laws or enforce laws that discriminate against us. We will not accept their law over us. There is a principle in the Christian faith that you can break a law if there's a greater law in jeopardy.

In 1972, a lesbian couple, an unmarried heterosexual couple, and my spouse and I, held a press conference in Los Angeles to announce to the police that we, each of the couples, had broken the laws of the State of California during the last weekend of May of that year.

The laws we broke were laws that forbid not only homosexual couples, but heterosexual couples even if they were married, from performing certain sex acts in the privacy of their own homes. Even though these sex acts were against the law, the police refused to arrest us. A friend actually made a citizen's arrest of us and took us to the police station where, again, the police refused to take us into custody. From there we were taken to the District Attorney's office. The District Attorney was on vacation. His office called him and he publicly announced to the press, that he would not enforce that part of the California Penal Code in Los Angeles County. Within three months, the California State Legislature recommended those laws, which had been on the books for over one hundred years, be abolished.

Only you can stop you from being a victim. It is so easy to allow old habits and patterns to dominate you. With freedom comes responsibility. We all can change to make the right choices in our lives.

Maybe that's why I love the following poem. It's called, "Autobiography in Five Chapters."

Chapter One

I walk down the street
There is a deep hole in the sidewalk
I fall in
I am lost....I am hopeless.
It isn't my fault.
It takes forever to find a way out.

Chapter Two

I walk down the same street.
There is a deep hole in the sidewalk.

I pretend I don't see it.
I fall in again.
I can't believe I'm in the same place.
But it isn't my fault.
It still takes a long time to get out.

Chapter Three

I walk down the same street.
There is a deep hole in the sidewalk.
I see it is there.
I still fall in.....it's a habit
My eyes are open
I know where I am
It is my fault.
I get out immediately.

Chapter Four

I walk down the same street.
There is a deep hole in the sidewalk.
I walk around it.

Chapter Five

I walk down another street.

By Portia Nelson, quoted in Charles L. Whitefield, M. D., Healing the Child Within (Orlando, Fl.: Health Communications, 1989).

As I have stated, you are in charge of the way you live your life. And you are in charge of your relationship with God.

Only you can open up your life to God. God created you so that you alone can decide if you will walk with God.

God is not heavy-handed. God will not break down the door to your heart. You have to let God in. You are in charge of your relationship with God.

I was ten years old when I invited God into my life consciously at the age of accountability. For me, the age of accountability came early. As I entered and passed through puberty and grew into adulthood, I was thankful that God was with me. I remember when I received my "call" to ministry. My aunt had prophesied, "Thus says God, "I am with you, and will keep you in all places where you go." For over fifty years of my life, God has been faithful to God's word. I really don't know what I would do if God was not in my life.

If you choose to open your life to God, there are some things you need to know about God. God is not a stern, angry judge only awaiting an opportunity somewhere to punish bad people who have failed to live a perfect life here on earth. As I have stated, God loves you more than you can comprehend.

God is not "the old man in the sky." God may have what we humans view as some human attributes, but God is not human. Jesus gave us two descriptions of God. One, "God is Spirit," and the other, "God is love."

If God is spirit, then I believe that God is life and intelligence existing entirely apart from physical embodiment. If God is love then all love in the universe is of God.

When Moses encountered God in the back side of the desert in Egypt as a voice coming out of the burning bush, God called him to lead the Israelites out of slavery. And Moses asked God a question: "If I come to the Israelites and tell them that the God of their foreparents has sent me to them and they ask me your name, what shall I say to them? God said to Moses, "I AM WHO I AM." Tell them that I AM has sent you to them." [Exodus 3: 13-14]

There is a wonderful hymn that we sing in Metropolitan Community Churches around the world – a hymn that describes some of the attributes of God. It's called, "When Israel Camped In Sinai."

"When Israel camped in Sinai,
God spoke and Moses heard,
This message tell the people, and give them this my word,
From Egypt I was with you; I bore you on my wing,
The whole of your great nation from slavery I did bring.
"Just as a mother eagle Who helps her young to fly,
I am a mother to you; your needs I will supply,
And you are as my children, my own who hear my voice,
I am a mother to you, the people of my choice.
If God is like an eagle Who helps her young to fly,
And God is also father, when what of you and I?
We have no fear of labels: we have no fear of roles,
God blends them and transcends them;
we seek the self same goals.
"Our God is not a woman; Our God is not a man.
Our God is both and neither; our God is I Who Am.
From all the roles that bind us, our God has set us free.
What freedom does God give us? the freedom just to be."

by Laurence G. Bermier (text copyright 1974 MCC)

We who are part of the Christian faith believe that Jesus is God in the flesh. We believe that almost two thousand years ago Jesus, the Christ, lived here on earth and still lives with us in the person of the Holy Spirit. I believe that everything in our lives must center on our relationship with God through faith in Jesus Christ. I am thankful that I opened my life to Christ because, in doing that, I became a new person. What I mean by that is God through Jesus gave me a new identity. I was no longer just Troy Perry. I became Troy Perry, heir and joint heir with Christ, part of a Holy nation.

I have shared with you how I came out as a gay male. I told you how I once believed the lie my childhood church had taught me – the lie that says God could not love me and that I could not be a Christian and homosexual. Because of that lie, I locked God out of my life. And that was the most awful time of my adult life. I know the difference now; I've been there! I want to remind you: Jesus came to take away your sins, not your sexuality. I believe if you have Christ, you have it all.

Remember throughout life: Always stay focused. The main thing is to keep the main thing the main thing!

CHAPTER EIGHT
There Is Only One Irreversible Law In The Universe.

It is interesting that almost all the world's religions teach this divine truth. Eastern religions call it karma, we Christians call it "reaping what you sow" [Ecclesiastes 11:1-10; Matthew 13:3; 16:25]. "Be not deceived; God is not mocked: for whatsoever a person sows, that shall they also reap. If a person sows to please their own wrong desires, they will be planting seeds of evil and they will surely reap a harvest of spiritual decay and death; But if a person plants the good things of the Spirit, they will reap the ever-lasting life which the Holy Spirit gives them. And let us not get tired of doing what is right, for after a while we will reap a harvest of blessing if we don't get discouraged and give up [Galatians 6:7-9].

Did California have it coming?

In January, 1994, hundreds of thousands of people were shocked out of their sleep by an earthquake that hit Los Angeles. My spouse and I woke to find our home shaking in that early morning. It is now history.

But our memories of that natural disaster – which claimed more than 50 lives, left thousands homeless and caused billions of dollars in damage – will long remain.

The Mother Church of our denomination was destroyed. Seventy-nine other churches of various denominations were also destroyed or badly damaged. A week after the earthquake, religion writer Larry Stammer of the Los

Angeles Times asked an editorial question: "Is Quake a Sign of God's Wrath?" Rev. Elder Nancy Wilson, pastor of our Mother Church, had been asked the very same question by some members of the church.

Interestingly, most of the religious leaders surveyed were not part of the California-had-it-coming school. Quite an opposite view was expressed by an Episcopal minister who offered his opinion that the first heart to break in such a tragedy is God's. A Jewish rabbi rejected any interpretation that would make God into "a monster, a force not for good but evil, a power that picks out tiny babies and old innocent women and deliberately bashes in their skulls."

But events like this do make us think, especially those of us who believe in a God of love.

Stammer wrote, "The cataclysms visited upon Southern California in the last several years-wildfires, riots, mudslides, drought and now earthquakes-can seem almost biblical in their dimension." An aide to Governor Pete Wilson said: "We call them plagues. And we're just two behind ancient Egypt – frogs and boils."

No shortage of voices claim that Southern California – perceived by some as a center of a lewd and licentious lifestyle – is the special target of God's wrath. A spokesperson for a leading televangelist speculated God may be lifting God's "hand of protection" for the United States. God, he said, is trying to "get our attention, for us as a nation to repent and pay attention to his Word." "God's telling us something," declared another church leader.

But is this true? Are the victims of disasters somehow the special targets of an angry God? In short, did California have it coming? Are the floods in Bangladesh, volcano eruptions in the Philippines, or war in Bosnia-Herzegovina gifts from an angry God?

To get some perspective, let's remember that in the time when Jesus lived, the world also had its share of unexplained disasters. In those days, most people thought that God punished only the wicked and always spared the righteous. Jesus Christ refuted this simplified notion in his own commentary on specific disasters of his day.

In one biblical story it is recorded that a tower fell on some people, perhaps after an earthquake. People wanted to know if God was punishing the people who had been killed.

Jesus answered, "Do you think that these Galileans were worse sinners than all the other Galileans because they suffered this way? I tell you, no!" And again he said, "Are those eighteen who died when the tower in Siloam fell on them – do you think they were more guilty than all the others living in Jerusalem? I tell you, no!" [Luke 13:2, 3a, 4, 5a]

The only other thing Jesus said in his commentary on this disaster was that we should always live our lives ready to mewt God when we die.

We understand today why California and other parts of the world have earthquakes, some places have floods, and still other places are susceptible to volcano eruptions. We study Earth Science (Physical Geography) which tells us that California has earthquakes because of continental drift and plate tectonics, that Bangladesh has floods because of its location and the weather systems which affect that part of the earth, and that the Philippines have volcanic eruptions because it is located in the "Ring of Fire" around the circumference of the Pacific Ocean.

Do we have it coming?

If I choose to live in Southern California, I take the chance of living with earthquakes. If I live in South Florida, I can expect to experience hurricanes on occasion. All of us make choices about where we live.

It is not necessarily God's fault or God's will if my home is destroyed in an earthquake or I lose my roof in Florida. I choose where I'll live. I must realize I cannot control earthquakes or the weather. In fact, Holy Scriptures tell us, "God, your heavenly parent, causes the sun to rise on good and bad alike, and sends the rain on the innocent and the wicked [Matthew 5:45b]."

I believe Mother Nature has her own set of rules that govern the way the earth reacts. However, I also believe that the way we human beings treat the earth can either cause Mother Nature to react benevolently or with hostility to human beings. I believe the Scriptures: We reap what we sow. The phenomenon of acid rain has become a major environmental concern in recent years. It is a complex problem that is far from completely understood, but seems to be caused largely by the combustion of fossil fuels. Human activities are altering the global temperature pattern. We have the start of a "Greenhouse Effect" warming on earth. We have all heard of El Nino, an ocean current with worldwide environmental implications. El Nino is considered by some experts to be the single most important disruptive influence on world climate patterns and has recently become a major topic for research by scientists in several fields according to the world press.

It is time for all humans to become environmentalists. Each of us has choices about the lives we lead and the environment in which we live.

SOWING THE SEEDS OF CHANGE.

On October 6, 1968, God gave me the words to sow in the larger world concerning God's love for all people, including the lesbian and gay community. I believe at that time it was God's will that we who were part of our community learned that we need no longer suffer from oppression sickness! Oppression sickness is an illness that allows others to define for you who you are and how you should feel about yourself. It invariably leads you to behave in a manner consistent with the oppressor's view of you.

I believe God was telling me, "See yourself as I desire you to be: healthy! Our first step toward the healing of oppression sickness is to ask the question, "How do I see myself?" We behave in ways consistent with the way we view ourselves. What we think of the person who looks back at us in the mirror largely determines our behavior in each day's events. If I only see myself as primarily a helpless victim that is what I will be. Being healed of oppression sickness means I must own my own feelings and take responsibility for myself. We can then say, "This is me."

God has given us the power – right now! – to become whatever we want to be; to feel as much love or anger or joy as we want to feel. It's all up to us.

So as we go about "sowing" in life, we must remember to "sow" for ourselves.

One of the most important things that you as a lesbian or gay male should be aware of is the way we should model wholeness, health, and holiness in our lives. In the early days of preaching in Metropolitan Community Church, I used to say, "We have to have more in our lives than the five "B's" – the bars, the baths, the bushes, the bookstores, and the beaches." That was my way of saying to the gay male community, "There is more to life than just sex." Twenty-seven years later, the Religious Right is still at work, trying to regulate our existence to that level. They want us to only be thought of as solely a vagina or penis, nothing more! Can you believe that? Well, we have a surprise for them; it's not true and we will not allow ourselves to be defined by their views. As I have already stated, never, never, never let other people define who you are.

God created you with mind, soul, and body. It is God's will that you model wholeness and balance in your life.

And you are in charge of your body. Don't abuse it; you only get one. Those of us with deep spiritual commitments should remember what the Apostle Paul wrote: "Do you not realize that your body is the temple of the Holy Spirit, who is in you and whom you received from God? For you have been purchased at a price. Therefore glorify God in your body." [1 Corinthians 6:19-20]

You are in charge of your soul and your spiritual body. You are both spirit and flesh. "And God formed the first human out of the dust of the ground and breathed into that person's nostrils the breath of life; and that person became a living soul." [Genesis 2:7] It is God's will that you choose to join your soul with God.

Jesus was asked one time what the greatest spiritual commandment is. Jesus said, "You shall love your God with all your heart, with all your soul, with all your mind, and with all your strength. The second is this: 'You shall love your neighbors as yourself." [Mark 12:30-31a]

You are in charge of what goes in your mind. Your brain is yours to control and you have to decide what goes into it. I'm one of those Christians who believes what we learn in this life we take with us into life eternal. "Let the same mind be in you that was in Christ Jesus." [Philippians 2:5]

Our minds can cause us to sow "unhealthy seeds" if our mindset differs from that of Jesus'. Unnatural fears can cause us to act out in some strange ways.

I remember years ago being invited to preach in a local MCC. As part of the weekend, I was told that I would speak to a college group. When I arrived at the school our secretary for the church told me, "Rev. Perry, the church board has asked me to tell you that you are not to use the name of our church in your address tonight."

I was shocked, to put it mildly!

"What did you say?" I asked. And I didn't ask very politely, quite frankly.

"I had nothing to do with it, Rev. Perry. The board is concerned that we might lose members of our church if the press knows you're here at our church," he said.

I couldn't believe my ears. First, I knew that the pastor of this church had been in the press numerous times to talk positively about our denomination. Second, I never invite the press into our local churches. If a church in our MCC denomination wishes to have press coverage about my visit, they can invite the press in, but I never do.

Having said all of that, I still could not believe what I had just been told. I thought, "My God, this church wants to keep us in the closet!" That thought made me mad. Really mad. Preachers are human, too, and feel all the human emotions. Including anger. And I would like to think my anger was what the Scriptures call "righteous anger."

Oh, I was angry. Both the Universal Fellowship of Metropolitan Community Churches and I have come too far to think that a local church in our denomination would ever consider not being fully open in the city where they are located.

I am sure the young man could read my body language because he looked like he thought I might strike him. Of course I would never do such a thing – but maybe he didn't know that.

Again he said, "Rev. Perry, I am only relaying a message."

"I understand that. I'll talk to you when I finish speaking," I said with a sense of finality.

Because I believe living in the closet is unhealthy for people and churches, I made sure that I peppered my speech with the name of our local church every thirty seconds.

When I finished, I told the secretary, "Now, I'd like you to call all the Board of Directors of the church and tell them I want them to join me for breakfast tomorrow morning. I'll pay for all of us to eat together so I can talk to them."

About that time the pastor of the church appeared, took one look at me and my body language, shrugged his shoulders and said, "I had nothing to do with the Board action."

"That's okay," I said as I told her what I had asked her secretary to do.

The next morning I met with the Board of Directors of

our church. I wasted no time. Right off the bat I asked them why they had sent the church secretary to tell me not to use the name of our church.

I said, "It made no sense to me, because your own pastor has been in the press over and over again and the name of the church is known all over this community."

"Well," one the Board of Directors said, "some of the members of the church were worried that they might lose their jobs if you came to preach because of the press coverage you would generate."

I shared with the Board what I had thought. "Have you seen the press around here?" I went on to tell the Board about how I had never called a press conference in one of our local churches. If a congregation wishes the press to be present in a church were I am speaking, they call the press conference, not me.

"How many church members were worried about my visit here?" I asked.

The Board members looked at one another. "Well," one answered, "only one. But she gives money to help the church."

"Wrong answer," I said without even really thinking. "We have left the spiritual closet behind and she has to do that, too, if she is going to live in the wholeness God wants her to. I want to talk to her."

I preached to a full church of our members on Friday night. The member with the job concerns was not present. Saturday night when I preached, we had standing room only. The member didn't come to that service, either. The

Sunday morning worship service arrived and still no member. Sunday night just before the service an usher came to my room and said, "The member with the job concerns is here."

When the sister came into the room the first thing she said to me was, "You are going to make me lose my job! I told the Board of Directors of the church that if they invited you here to preach the press would be here and that I would lose my job."

"Sister," I asked, "do you see the press here?"

Ignoring my question, she said again, "You are going to make me lose my job."

"I can assure you," I said, "that you are not going to lose your job because I am preaching in your church. The press is not here!"

This sister refused to hear my words. Again she said, "You are going to make me lose my job. I am a child psychiatrist and if the state knew I am a member of Metropolitan Community Church they would fire me. Because you are here, I am going to lose my job! Nobody knows I'm a lesbian but they will now because the Board invited you here."

I was shocked and angered by the sister's words. I could not believe her unreasonable fear. And she was not listening to the truth. She was creating and sowing the seeds that would sprout and grow into her own fear and destruction.

"Sister," I said very quietly, "you are correct. You are going to lose your job. Not because I have visited your church, but because you are creating the loss of your job with your fear. The Bible tells me that Job, someone who loved God, said after he had lost his children and all his wealth, 'What I feared has come upon me; what I dreaded has happened to me' [Job 3:25]. Based on this spiritual law of the universe, you're right! You will lose your job."

The women screamed at me, "You are going to make me lose my job. Nobody knows I'm a lesbian."

Before I thought, I responded, "Sister, everybody knows you are a lesbian! I have never met a more butch woman in high heels in my life! Everybody knows you are a lesbian!"

Now let me ask you: How do you see yourself?

The Bible says, "As a person thinks, so they are." I believe every human has to own their feelings and take responsibility for them. We can determine within ourselves whether to be angry, to hurt, to love, to care, to stay on a job or to leave it. We can not allow ourselves to cop out with, "You are going to make me lose my job" or "They did this to me" or "She makes me angry" or "He makes me unhappy" or "He causes me pain." God does not want us to be a product of what people have done or are now doing to us. I believe with God's help we have the power to become whatever we want to be; to feel as much love or anger or joy as we want to feel. We can sow it and we can reap it. It's up to us, no one else.

What makes you uniquely you? What made Mary the mother of Jesus to be Mary the mother of Jesus? One thing: The fact that she found the will of God and did it. If Mary had refused the call of God to be impregnated by the Holy Spirit, if Mary had felt to raise her son, if Mary had not become a member of the Christian faith, then she would not have been Mary. What we are is related to what we choose to do. God created us and created us with a purpose. As we discover the purposes of God, and begin to fulfill them, that is the process of knowing who you are.

For some of us who look to God and walk with Christ, the images of men, women, and children dealing with AIDS, refugees crowding the borders of a country at war, or innocent people gasping for breath after a terrorist attack is deeply disturbing. The unasked, but ever-present question is: Where was the God they trusted as such atrocities happened?

Elie Wiesel tells of how a young boy was hanged in Auschwitz while others were forced to watch. Someone in the horrified crowd asked, "Where is God?" Another person answered that God was there, hanging on that tree.

God is also there, with AIDS patients, refugees, and everyone else who suffers. Christ has told us that how we respond to strangers is how we respond to him. Jesus identified himself with their plight. "I was a stranger and you took me in. . . As you did it to one of the least of these my followers, you did it to Me" [Matthew 25:35, 40].

Always remember friends, we reap what we sow!

CHAPTER NINE
YOUR SEXUALITY IS A GIFT FROM GOD.

In the beginning, God created sex.

And God created us as sexual human beings.

Members of the Jewish, Christian, and Islamic faiths believe the book of Genesis in the Bible contains the story of the first persons created by God: Adam and Eve. There were two functions of sex within the human family: to give pleasure and sometimes to create children. The Jews did not look at sex as a nuisance or a problem to be endured. The average person in ancient times appears to have had a normal, healthy, enjoyable sex life. Unfortunately much of the biblical discussion about sex focuses on its problems.

A few of the subjects that concern people in our day were considered non-issues during Bible times. For instance, since there was little time between puberty and marriage, the ancient writers ignored the question of masturbation. Nowhere in the Hebrew or Christian scriptures does the Bible say masturbation is a sin.

The attitudes about sex differed greatly according to the times and the circumstances.

Many people in the Christian Faith believe that sin entered the world as a result of the disobedience of Adam and Eve to God's command not to eat the fruit of the tree of knowledge of good and evil.

The biblical story goes like this:

After God created the world and all that is in it, God planted a beautiful garden in Eden. God then created Adam and placed him in the garden to take care of it. In the garden were various trees that were delightful to look at and good for food, with the tree of life in the middle of the garden and the tree of knowledge of good and evil. God told Adam that he was free to eat from any of the trees in the garden except the tree of knowledge of good and evil.

"The moment you eat from it you are surely doomed to die," God said.

Sometime later, according to the biblical account, God created Eve and placed her in the garden with Adam. All goes well until one day a serpent speaks to the first human beings. The serpent disputes what God has said about the tree of knowledge.

"The only reason God does not want you eating the fruit from that tree is that God knows your eyes will be open to what is good and bad and you will become gods, too," said the cunning serpent.

Adam and Eve eat the fruit. The first thing they realized was that they were naked. The first thing they did was make themselves some clothes. And then they hid from God.

God comes walking in the garden in the cool of the day, but cannot find Adam and Eve. God calls out to them and finally they answered.

"We heard you in the garden; but we are afraid, because we are naked, so we hid ourselves."

God listens as Adam and Eve tell their story of their encounter with the serpent and how they came about to eat the fruit from the tree of knowledge.

The Genesis story tells us that God cursed the serpent for its part in deceiving Adam and Eve. Then God sends them out of the garden in Eden. Because of their act of disobedience sin entered the world. Christians call this act, "The Fall."[Genesis 1-3]

Fundamentalist Christians believe that homosexuals came into being as a result of the fall of humanity. Their argument is that heterosexuality was the norm until Adam and Eve sinned and then human sexuality was distorted.

Of course, the Bible does not say that at all. I believe that Adam and Eve were the first persons created by God. I do not believe they were the only ones created by God. I believe that God in God's wisdom created a wonderful group of human beings of all races as well as sexual orientations. In fact, the Bible, if you read it seriously, lets us know that.

After the fall of Adam and Eve, the Bible tells us they gave birth to two sons, Cain and Abel. Cain murdered his brother Abel. If God did not create other human beings, then the human race would have ended there; but the Bible tells us that Cain left his parents and went to the land of Nod where he took a wife who gave birth to their son, Enoch.

The Bible does not imply that Adam and Eve had a daughter who married her brother, as some fundamentalist Christians believe. Cain's wife came from the other families of human beings God created [Genesis 4: 16-17].

We who are part of MCC believe that human sexuality, of which homosexuality is part, is a gift of God.

In 1979, the General Conference of the Universal Fellowship of Metropolitan Community Churches adopted the following statement of our Commission on Faith, Fellowship, and Order:

> "This church came into existence affirming that homosexuality is a valid manifestation of the divine creation of human beings in the image and likeness of God. Thus, sexuality is a gift from God. From the beginning, Metropolitan Community Church has preached that gay people, along with all people, share the benefits of God's grace.
>
> Jesus taught by his example that human sexuality is to be dealt with in the same way as any other aspect of humanness...The unique emphasis of Metropolitan Community Church is dealing with human sexuality openly and honestly as Jesus did. Instead of repressing, denying, or hiding sexuality, Metropolitan Community Church follows the pattern of Jesus and puts it on par with other aspects of humanness.
>
> Metropolitan Community Church realizes that God fully intended for human beings to be human and sexual and that sexuality should be an integral part of the wholeness of a fully human person.
>
> Thus, Metropolitan Community Church attempts to defuse the tension caused by relegating sexuality to a separate realm. This leaves room for redirecting the energy thus saved into efforts for the responsible use of sexuality as Jesus did...Putting a lot of energy into suppressing one area of life impedes the liberation of the whole person. Therefore, we consider that defusing tension in the area of sexuality will result in release of immense amounts of energy for living a fully Christian life...We recognize that sexuality is an essential aspect of our personhood, an aspect that cannot be ignored or separated from the rest of our humanness. By this, Metropolitan Community Church is emphasizing that we cannot find spiritual, mental, or physical wholeness unless we deal affirmatively with our sexuality.
>
> But, our sexuality is not and should not be the focal point of our lives. An important emphasis in the Christian ministry of Metropolitan Community Church is that everything in our life,

including our sexuality, must center on our relationship with God through faith in Jesus Christ. Metropolitan Community Church emphasizes that sexuality is part of the whole self which is called into a relationship with God who is the Creator, Redeemer, and Sustaining Spirit."

I remember a long day in San Francisco where the Governing Board of the National Council of Churches was meeting. The delegation from our denomination was questioned about MCC's theology. Every question was about sex. For over an hour we politely answered the questions. Finally, a delegate from the National Council said to us, "All you people want to talk about is sex."

"But that's all you've wanted to talk about. It's you who have been asking the questions," our delegation said.

The Universal Fellowship of Metropolitan Community Churches is dismayed that so much time and energy are spent on the issue of homosexuality, and calls on the larger Christian church to move beyond its current obsession with that one part of sexuality and envision a Theology of Human Sexuality, that will encompass heterosexuality, homosexuality, and the full spectrum of human sexuality, so that at long last the Christian church can say, as God did when God created humankind with sex organs, "It is good."

Sex is God's good gift. A theological framing of sexuality depends, then, not only on our understanding of the church and of sanctification, but on our understanding of sexuality itself and of the way it does or does not define our lives before God.

We need a theology of human sexuality that gives sex its due while putting it into the larger context of the Christian life. The last thing we need is a repressive sexuality that results in destructive shame. Having said that, still we must remember, human sexual behavior is never free from the potential for misuse.

As Augustine noted in his writings on marriage, the desire for sexual fulfillment inevitably leads to moments of deception and manipulation. Even in the best of sexual relationships, we cannot avoid moments in which we hurt each other, however unintentionally. The vulnerability that accompanies sexual expression is a source of intimacy but also an occasion of misunderstanding, even exploitation.

The writers of the Bible only concerned themselves with homosexuality as it was exhibited in only two things: cult prostitution and pederasty.

The pagan religions that surrounded and contaminated Israel's history practiced various forms of cult prostitution, usually centered on the theme of fertility. If a farmer wanted larger crops or greater flocks, he needed to appeal to the fertility gods; should a wife want to bear children the same appeal was necessary.

One means of pleasing the fertility gods was to engage in sex with male or female prostitutes available at the temple. As bizarre as this may sound, the practice was common; it endured into New Testament times and frequently was assimilated into worship ritual.

Pagan ceremonies and celebrations could become riotous and gruesome. A great deal of wine was frequently consumed as tribute to Baal for good crops. The sacrifice of children to Molech, or Chemosh, the Moabite God, also occurred.

During the time of the judges, the Jews adopted many of the practices of the fertility cults (Judg. 8:33) despite the fact the Law strictly prohibited them (Deut. 23:17-18). However, these were only the beginning of their disobedience. Eventually half the tribe of Manasseh accepted the religion of prostitution(1Chron. 5:25).

Not everyone participated in the temple prostitution cult worship, but everyone would have been aware of its presence. These cult practices remained common in certain areas of the world well through the time of Christ and Paul.

The writers of the Bible were concerned with cult homosexual prostitution, because this was their primary contact with homosexuality, not homosexual relationships as we know them today.

Paul's condemnation in Scripture (Rom. 1:23-27; 1 Cor. 6:9; 1 Tim. 1:9-10) was against cult temple homosexual prostitution and adults defiling children sexuality.

Outside of prohibitions about the misuse of God's gift of sexuality, the Bible gives no restrictions on how people may enjoy sex. For example, there is no discussion or prohibitions on married sexual practices anywhere in the Bible. What you do in your bedroom is your business. God gives you "free will" to practice sex in all of its different expressions.

Paul's treatment of the subject is especially enlightening (1 Cor. 7:1-7), for he argued that regular sexual intercourse was essential for a couple. It was the couple's duty to please each other. He recommended self-control but recognized the necessity of physical satisfaction. This demonstrates that sex was appreciated as a source of pleasure. Couples frequently enjoyed sex without guilt, with no intention of having children from their union. This was especially important considering the sexual temptations present in the society around them. The text also suggests that it was perfectly acceptable for a couple to admit their need for sex. Paul discusses this as normal and expects the wise couple to honor that need.

The Scriptures give some guidelines on sex that were commended to the early Christians. Couples were expected to exercise enough self-control so they could carry out their normal responsibilities. For instance, Paul acknowledged a couple's right to refrain from sex in order to devote themselves to prayer. He also insisted that marriage partners not use sex solely for their own satisfaction. They were responsible, rather, to also meet the needs of their partner (1Cor.7:1-7).

The Song of Solomon is remarkably bold in its use of sexual expressions and imagery. Those familiar with this work were exposed to very intimate details about the subject. The author admires his lover's breasts (4:5; 7:3-7), and is enamored by her delectable kisses (4:11). She in turn loves his tender embraces (8:3), and delights in his sweet mouth (5:16) and marvelous legs (5:15). This sensuous book speaks frankly of the sexual experience as an accepted part of Jewish culture.

Self-control and making good choices in your life are major themes in the Bible, and lust is one of the passions which is to be held in check. The word "lust" or strong desire can be applied to a wide range of subjects, including food and ambition (1Tim.3:1), as well as sex. In ancient society, as today, there were multiplied invitations to surrender to illicit sexual desires. Jesus warned us against capitulating to those lusts (Matt. 5:28).

The Bible's prohibitions about sex always have to do with the misuse of God's gift. The Bible tells us that we should never push one's self on another person who is not interested in us. To sexually harass anyone is wrong. To rape another person is a sin.

I'm often asked, "What about single gay Christians who are not in long-term relationships? What acts are permissable for us?"

While I respect the question, may I lovingly suggest it is the wrong question? It begins in the wrong place.

True expressions of Christian spirituality never begin with externals - such as sexual acts. A true understanding of Christian spirituality begins in our hearts and minds. At MCC, we believe God's Word teaches that sexual ethics are far more important than sexual acts.

Sexual ethics ask a very helpful series of foundational questions: Is my sexual expression loving? Is it mutual? Is it caring? Is it free of coercion or the misuse of power? Is it free of manipulation? Is it honest?

These internal issues are far, far more important than questions about specific sexual acts. Answer the internal questions in a healthy, positive way and the external questions take care of themselves.

The Bible gives no restrictions on ways consenting adults should go about enjoying their sexuality. There are no prohibitions on consensual sexual practices. You will discover what a joy the human body is and how it gives you wonderful pleasure.

What you do in your bedroom is your business, not the business of the Church, the community, or the government so long as it is with another consenting adult. You should never have to explain your sex acts to any one. You should always view your sexuality as a holy gift from God.

Praise God for your sexuality and "sing aloud upon your bed!" (Psalms 149:5)

CHAPTER TEN
Never For The Sake Of Peace And Quiet Deny Your Own Existence.

I opened the Bible and read a passage from Matthew chapter 28 in which Jesus teaches about baptism. Then I looked at Paul.

"Do you have Jesus Christ as your Savior?"

"Yes," he answered.

"Is it your sincere desire to be baptized?"

"Yes, sir."

"Have you asked God's forgiveness for all sins you have committed, whether knowingly or unknowingly?"

"Yes, I have."

"In Metropolitan Community Churches, we baptize by sprinkling, pouring, or full immersion. How do you wish to be baptized?" I asked.

"Just like the other prisoners," he answered. "By immersion."

I placed one hand on his back and I took his hands in my other hand and there in a prison setting his body slipped beneath the baptismal waters as I uttered the ancient words, "Buried with Christ in baptism... raised to walk in newness of life."

Two weeks earlier I reached across my desk and picked up a letter from the stack of incoming mail. Before I even opened the envelope, I knew I was holding in my hands a letter from a prisoner. I long ago learned that the added numbers in the return address indicate an inmate's prison number.

Over the past three decades, I've received thousands and thousands of letters from people in every walk of life – people who are struggling to reconcile their spiritual faith with their sexual orientation. I've received letters from business leaders, actors and actresses, clergy people, students, grandfathers and grandmothers, and high school students. I've received letters from people of immense wealth and people who were homeless and without so much as a return address. I've received letters from people on every continent around the globe. But perhaps no letters touch me as deeply as the ones I regularly receive from prison inmates.

I pulled the rumpled paper from the envelope and carefully read the handwritten note. It was from an inmate at Chino Men's Correctional Facility – a California men's prison located an hour-and-a-half east of my Los Angeles-based office.

The letter tugged at my heart. It was from a 60-year-old inmate whom I'll call Paul, to protect his identity. He was a gay man who was serving time for a crime for which he took full responsibility. He acknowledged the wrong he had done and was paying his debt to society.

But while in prison, a remarkable thing had happened.

Paul had time to reflect on his life – and he came to see that something was missing. Paul's difficult experience behind prison bars gave him an opportunity to review his life. (Never forget that God is at work in your life – even in the most difficult and painful circumstances.)

And that's where the miracle happened! Sitting in a prison cell beneath the heat of the California desert, Paul experienced a spiritual rebirth. His faith in God was reborn. He began to pray. He started to read his Bible and to apply its spiritual lessons to his life.

Now this is a key point: Nothing in Paul's external life changed. But inside – in his mind and his spirit and his emotional life – Paul found a deep sense of forgiveness and peace.

One day Paul read in his Bible that Christian believers observed a spiritual rite known as baptism. Christians in different faith groups practice baptism differently – some by total immersion, some by sprinkling, some by pouring. No matter how baptism is observed, it has two purposes.

First, it is a public way of demonstrating that a believer has embraced the Christian faith and is a follower of Jesus Christ. And, second, it is intended to be a ritual that signifies a believer has ended old, self-centered ways of living, has been washed in God's forgiveness, and is ready to live a life dedicated to the teachings of Jesus Christ.

Well, Paul took his faith seriously – even behind prison bars. So he went to the prison chaplain, explained his spiritual faith and asked the chaplain to do for Paul what the chaplain had done for other Christian inmates. He asked the chaplain to baptize him in the Christian faith.

The chaplain looked at him for a moment and then he said one word: "No."

Paul sat there stunned. Was it possible that his chaplain was refusing to allow him to take the next step in his Christian faith?

"You are an unrepentant homosexual," the chaplain continued. "Until you turn away from your homosexuality, I won't baptize you."

"But Chaplain, I believe this is the way God created me and I don't believe God made a mistake when God created my life," Paul said.

Paul went back to his cell. The pain of rejection stung him. He began to pray– and then he had another idea.

"I'll write to my family's minister. He knows my family. Surely he'll help me take the next step in my Christian faith. Surely he will come baptize me," he thought.

And his family minister also refused to baptize him. "We don't baptize homosexuals," he said.

Imagine Paul's added pain. All he wanted to do was to follow his spiritual faith – and everywhere he turned he experienced rejections. The Church – the very institution that should reflect Chris's unconditional love and acceptance – is turning Paul away.

But thank God, Paul was resourceful. And he had perseverance. He didn't take "no" for a final answer. He didn't give up.

So on this particular morning, I am holding his letter in my hands and I am reading his story.

"Rev. Perry, I am writing to ask if you will come to Chino Correctional Facility and baptize me."

My heart went out to Paul. I was preparing for a busy travel and preaching schedule and knew I couldn't perform the baptism myself. I started to forward Paul's letter to one of our MCC ministers – but something inside stopped me.

I learned that when I experience what I call the "inner witness," I need to stop what I am doing and pray. I've learned to listen to the "still, small voice" inside. This is often the way I find God's guidance in my life.

And that's exactly what I did. I set the letter aside. I prayed for Paul and I asked God for guidance.

And the next morning when I walked into my office, I knew in my heart that God wanted me to perform Paul's baptism.

The arrangements were made. On the appointed day, Frank Zerilli, my longtime assistant, and I made the hour-and-a-half drive into the California desert.

We pulled up to the Chino prison. The desert heat was sweltering under an azure blue sky. I made my way across the parking lot, entered the front doors and asked for the chaplain.

Now, I've been involved in jail and prison ministries for more than 30 years – but I never get used to the sound of clanging metal doors, the jingle of keys opening and locking doors, the prison buzzer that announces doors are being opened.

The chaplain approached and we shook hands. We exchanged pleasantries. But inside, I kept thinking about the pain and rejection Paul had felt from this minister.

"Chaplain," I said. "I am confused. I want to understand something. Is it true that you have refused to baptize Paul, even though he has expressed his faith in Jesus Christ?"

"Yes," he answered. "He refused to stop being a homosexual and he's not even trying to stop."

Well, I knew I wasn't going to let this go.

"Rev. Perry," the chaplain continued, "we're not properly

equipped with a baptismal pool or baptismal font in this prison. Some of the inmates are filling a large laundry cart with water. That's where the baptism will take place."

I asked for a Bible and one was brought to me. Then Paul was escorted into the room where the chaplain, Paul, and I waited for the laundry cart to be filled.

A jumble of thoughts ran through my mind. I thought of the tens of thousands of gays and lesbians I have ministered to who were also rejected by their churches. I thought of all the people who still don't know that even though the church may reject them, God still loves them unconditionally. I thought of hundreds of other prisoners with whom I have corresponded over the years. And I thought about the pain Paul had felt and the rejection he had experienced by this chaplain.

I turned to the chaplain. "I just have to keep talking about this," I said. "You are the only Protestant chaplain for this section of the prison and this inmate has expressed his sincere spiritual faith and commitment. And you still refuse to baptize this man?"

"Yes, Rev. Perry, I will not baptize him," he replied.

Paul spoke up and reminded me that his family minister had also refused to baptize him.

I now turned my full attention to Paul. This was his moment and his event. "Well, Paul," I said, "I have to be honest with you. My tax money doesn't pay your family minister. But it does pay the salary of this chaplain."

The chaplain piped up, "Rev. Perry, under California law we're not required to do anything that violates our own convictions."

Now, those who know me well know its not my nature to keep quiet about these matters.

"Well, chaplain, I have to respect your personal convictions," I said. "So I'll also have to share my personal convictions with you. I am just shocked by this. I can't understand how any minister can refuse a sincere spiritual request. I'm afraid I'm going to have to give you a little publicity on this situation."

As I finished these words, there was a knock at the door and an inmate informed us that the laundry cart turned baptismal pool was filled and ready. We stepped out and sure enough there it was – a large laundry cart had literally been filled with water and was to serve as the baptismal pool. Other inmates joined us.

For just a second it dawned on me: Given these arrangements, there was no way to keep my suit from becoming very wet. And as quickly as the thought entered my mind, it left. Suddenly I didn't care. This was about Paul, and about Paul's faith, and about his faithful witness to God's calling on his life.

Paul crawled into the laundry cart and I was ready to perform the service when Paul spoke up. Suddenly he asked the most disconcerting question – a question that stopped me in my tracks.

"Rev. Perry, am I an abomination? What does it mean to be an abomination?" he asked.

I was stunned. "Why do you ask that?" I inquired.

"Almost every day since I have been in prison, people tell me I am abomination because I am gay. Is that true?"

I felt the lump in my throat tighten and tears well in my eyes.

"No, Paul. You are not an abomination. God created you as you are and God loves you as you are. Paul, when I get back to my office, I'm going to mail you some more pamphlets so you can better understand just how much God loves you and so you can stay strong in your Christian faith."

Now, I tell you the truth: If I live to be 100, I'll never forget the sight that surrounded us in the moment – or the sense of God's presence and peace in that place. There we were behind prison walls. An inmate was standing in a laundry cart filled with water. A chaplain who had refused to help looked on. Other inmates gathered to watch the service. And in the midst of this very strange scene, we were overwhelmed with God's peace and presence.

I placed one hand on his back and I took his hands in my other hand and there in a prison setting his body slipped beneath the baptismal waters as I uttered the ancient words, "Buried with Christ in baptism... raised to walk in newness of life."

And I will tell you this: I was overwhelmed – almost transformed! – by the moment. The sense of spiritual awe was so powerful I could well have been standing in one of the world's great, impressive cathedrals. Yet here I was, surrounded by block walls and concrete floors and I was overwhelmingly aware of God's presence.

Paul stepped out of the makeshift baptismal pool and he, too, was overwhelmed by God's grace and goodness. He was dripping wet and without even pausing to think, he reached out and grabbed me and hugged me. He held on tight as the water ran down my shirt and trousers and I didn't mind for a second.

This was a holy moment!

This was a transformational moment!

This was a life-changing moment!

And I thought: This is why this church exists. This is why God has blessed Metropolitan Community Churches. This is what we are called to do. As long as we proclaim Christ's message of hope and faith and forgiveness to people who are hurting or seeking or rejected, MCC's work is not finished.

Indeed, I've often thought that we in Metropolitan Community Churches share something in common with the song from "The Man of La Mancha." We, too, have been called to march through hell for a heavenly cause.

My testimony is that it has all been worth it. Every step has been worth it.

Like Paul, we can all find these life-changing moments. Never for the sake of peace and quiet deny your own existence. During our lifetime we are born and reborn, only to experience new and different ways of living. We can always change.

Jesus said in Christian Scripture "Ask, and it shall be given you; seek, and you shall find; knock, and it shall be opened unto you" (Matthew 7:7). In the south of the United States where I was born, we have an old saying that sounds a lot like Scripture, "The squeaky wheel gets the most grease." I believe with all of my heart that it is not enough in the spiritual realm for people of faith to simply pray for something. As much as I believe in the power of prayer, I also believe we must put legs on our prayers. This means we must put action to our prayers. Our actions create the open doors through which God works. And sometimes "putting feet to our prayers" means we are required to speak up and to speak out.

I learned a long time ago even well-meaning people in government could not understand the importance of GLBT rights unless someone talked to them and raised their consciousness of the issues. The title of this chapter is an adaptation of the words of Dag Hammerskold, one of the first presidents of the United Nations. Hammerskold was a gay man in a time when most of the world's cultures still didn't understand homosexuality. Yet Dag Hammerskold lives today in the memory of the world for his life's work of bringing humankind together and promoting peace among the nations.

One of the amazing things about reaching my age (I'm 62 at this writing) and being an individual who has been a part of the modern gay rights movement in America and the world, I have learned how important this chapter title is. I learned a long time ago, just as many of you have, that I must refuse to accept the status quo in my life. I'm amazed at how much has changed in our world over the past few decades – all because so many people have refused to deny our own existence in exchange for peace and quiet. If you are serious about living a liberated life, one of the most important things you can do with your life is to be yourself and to live your life with openness and authenticity. All external change in our world begins first with internal change and internal acceptance. And we will never end the external oppression in our world until we first end our internal oppressions.

There are many ways in which I try to live out my own commitment to openness and authenticity. Many years ago, when I came to realize that God had created me as a gay man – along with the realization that all of God's creation is good – I also realized that I, along with all my gay, lesbian, bisexual and transgender brothers and sisters, deserve to be treated just as everyone else is in my culture. I hope deep inside you believe that, too. But this commitment has also placed obligations on my life: I consciously carry with me the obligation to help my culture understand who I am. Lives lived in openness and authenticity help to bring understanding and healing to our societies.

So I've spent these past 35 years praying for a greater societal understanding of GLBT people. And I've put "legs to my prayers." By God's grace, I've been willing to take a stand. To speak up. To pay the price. To not be silent. To persevere.

Let me say a personal word to you: If the thought of living your life in complete openness and authenticity is a fearful thought for you, let me offer some words of encouragement. Over time, it not only becomes easier to live with openness and authenticity – it actually becomes a natural part of life, and brings emotional and spiritual health into our lives.

Let me share with you some experiences from my own life and ministry and activism. These are experiences that brought profound changes because I put feet to my prayers. I took action and responsibility. I refused to keep my mouth shut.

For many centuries Christian churches and denominations used the six "clobber passages" of the Bible to condemn GLBT Christians. But when God called me to begin Metropolitan Community Churches in 1968 I had three life-changing spiritual insights.

First, God gave me an inner conviction that God's gay and lesbian children were loved and welcomed by God. God's Word in the Epistle to the Romans 8:16 became real to me: "The Spirit of God bears witness with our spirit, that we are the children of God."

Second, I knew that churches had held biblical interpretations – sometimes for centuries – that they later came to see as misinterpretations. Sadly, this happened with the biblical justification of slavery, the oppression of women, and acceptance of racism. In each of these cases, the Church came to admit that centuries of biblical interpretation were in error.

Third, I knew how easy it was for people to read their prejudices and biases into God's Word – rather than letting God's Word speak its own truth.

In the early days of Metropolitan Community Churches, I made a commitment – a commitment to study God's Word and find out what the Scriptures really said about homosexuality. And one other thing is worth noting: I was committed to following this research wherever it took me. I had no desire to use Scripture to justify my beliefs – I wanted to align my life with God's will and God's heart.

So I plunged into my research.

I participated in debates. I read biblical commentaries. I met with theologians. I studied the writings of Jewish rabbis and commentaries on the Hebrew Scriptures by Jewish theologians and historians. I read books on the science and theories of biblical interpretation.

Early members of Metropolitan Community Churches began to form interpretations based on the latest scholarship and the cultural context of biblical days.

Out of this research, the founding members and ministers of Metropolitan Community Churches became convinced that the six "clobber passages" traditionally used against gays and lesbians had been interpreted out of context. Past church leaders had read their own biases into the verses.

For the past 35 years, Metropolitan Community Churches have challenged the Church to re-examine God's Word as it relates to homosexuality. Thanks to the boldness, faithfulness and ministry of those early MCCers, the role of gays, lesbians, bisexuals and transgender persons in the Church has moved to the forefront of almost every Christian denomination.

Together, we have forever changed the face of Christianity.

One of the greatest significant theological breakthroughs in my 35 years of ministry with Metropolitan Community Churches happened in 2002 when the New Oxford Annotated Bible 3rd Edition came off the press.

This ecumenical study Bible contains the Revised Standard Version of the Bible. This new edition was supervised by Oxford University with study and research notes edited by the world's outstanding biblical scholars.

This is the world's premier study Bible – and in a major breakthrough for GLBT people of faith everywhere – its footnotes and study materials incorporate many of MCC's biblical interpretations and views.

In the new study Bible, the views and interpretations of

the "clobber passages" use the theology and interpretations we have developed within MCC.

Imagine the joy I felt when I recently opened a package from a scholar, educator and friend to find a copy of The New Oxford Annotated Bible, Third Edition – along with a handwritten inscription that read, "Dear Rev. Perry: Thanks for your life and ministry which have helped to shape the scholarship of this edition. May God continue to bless you and Metropolitan Community Churches in your quest for truth."

Let me share a few illustrations with you from various verses in this Bible:

– For 35 years, we have been teaching that the sin of Sodom and Gomorrah, understood in the Jewish context of that day, was the sin of severe inhospitality to strangers. This interpretation appears in The New Oxford Annotated Bible.

– In Jude 7, this version offers the alternate reading that the people of Sodom and Gomorrah "went after other flesh" - leading to the interpretation that their sin was against angelic visitors, not other humans, and thus could not be a reference to homosexuality.

– In Romans 1, the footnotes in the new version indicate that this passage is used "to denote not the orientation of sexual desire, but its immoderate indulgence," that is, it is not a prohibition of God's gift, but a prohibition against its misuse.

– 1 Corinthians 6:9-10 adopts MCC's interpretation that these verses prohibit temple prostitution - not homosexuality.

– The Leviticus passage is the least clear – though it is set in the larger context of differentiating the Children of Israel from the hostile nations that surrounded them.

All in all, the world-renowned biblical scholars who prepared The New Oxford Annotated Bible have adopted a great deal of MCC's own scholarship and theology, i.e. there is no biblical condemnation of homosexuality – only prohibitions against its misuse, just as there is no biblical blanket condemnation of heterosexuality, only prohibitions against misuse of that gift.

The publication of this version of the Bible marked a profound advancement for all GLBT people of faith – all because we didn't accept the status quo... because we dared to question... and because we dared to speak out.

Another area where I have invested a great deal of my life – where I have put "feet to my prayers" – is in obtaining equal marriage rights for GLBT persons as those afforded under the law for heterosexual couples.

In December of 1968, three months after founding the Metropolitan Community Churches, a young Latino couple approached me and asked if I would be willing to perform a wedding ceremony for them. Today, as I write these words, MCC clergy perform more than 5000 same-sex weddings every year. But it was almost an unheard of in 1968. I said yes – and this wedding ceremony, even though not legally recognized under the laws of the State of California, was blessed in the sight of God and became the first same-sex wedding performed by Metropolitan Community Churches.

Hundreds of couples followed after that. In 1970, a lesbian couple approached me and asked if I would marry them. During our counseling session, one of the women looked at me and asked, "Rev. Perry, why can't our marriage be recognized by the government?"

And I said, "You're exactly right. Why not?" And with that, on June 12, 1970, I performed the wedding of Neva Joy Heckman and Judith Ann Belew.

But this ceremony was different from all of our previous wedding services because it was conducted under a provision of California law that allowed a common law liaison to be formalized by a religious ceremony. This law was written in colonial California times and was placed in the code of California law so that unmarried couples who were not close to a church or courthouse, but whose relationship was understood by the community where people lived to be that of a marriage, could quietly go to a clergyperson who could marry them and then notify the court clerk that the marriage had taken place. The couple did not have to purchase a marriage license as other couples did; they received the same legal recognition that their marriage had taken place. The clerk was obligated under California law to file the certification from me as the officiating clergyperson and formally declare this a marriage.

In accordance with the law, I mailed the certification to the County Clerk in Los Angeles where all three of us resided. The clerk refused to accept my certification. With that, I put legs on my prayers and in concert with the couple, we sued the State of California to show cause why the State of California would not accept my certification of the couple as married.

And you know what happened? We lost the battle – but we won the war. We lost the battle: The court considered the case and found that the marriage was not legal because the California statute specifically stated that marriage must be between a man and a woman. But I also know we won the war: We moved the debate over equal marriage rights for same-sex partners to the forefront.

Our Metropolitan Community Churches have kept the marriage debate before the media and the politicians as an equal right we expect as citizens in our culture.

Our Church continues to marry couples as we've always done – and we have held same-sex wedding ceremonies in public and highly visible forums. We relentlessly challenge our culture's view of marriage. At the Second March on Washington for GLBT rights in America in 1987, Metropolitan Community Churches helped organize and participated in "The Wedding," a highly visible demonstration for marriage of same-sex couples.

We held this public ceremony again at the Third March on Washington in 1993 and yet again at the Millennium March on Washington for Equality in April of 2000. More than 3000 couples participated in this ceremony in front of the Lincoln Memorial – and the event was covered by CNN, the BBC, MSNBC, CNBC, the New York Times, the Washington Post, the Associated Press and Reuters News Service.

MCC was the first religious organization to include same-sex unions and wedding ceremonies for gays and lesbians in its bylaws. Today many religious groups perform services of holy union and marriage for same-sex couples – but only one religious organization outside Metropolitan Community Churches has voted as an entire organization to recognize and validate same-sex ceremonies: the Unitarian-Universalist Association.

People used to ask me, "Why are you butting your head

against the wall over this issue? It will never happen." But guess what? So many people in our communities around the world didn't give up the fight for this right. As of this writing, two countries have given full marriage rights to same sex couples – Holland and Denmark. And France and Germany have adopted legal protections that provide more than 90% equivalency to heterosexual marriage rights.

Before I die, my prayer is that I might legally marry my partner and spouse of 17 years, Phillip Ray De Blieck. And I will continue to put legs to my prayers. Because I believe that with God ALL things are possible.

So my testimony – my witness – is that prayer makes a difference in our world. When we lift our prayers to God and then stand up and speak out, we unleash God's power and presence. I can't say this enough.

Let me share another example.

In 1960, I was expelled from the Christian Bible college in which I was enrolled in Chicago, Illinois for being gay. I was told by college authorities that I was "not fit to be educated in a Christian school." Then life set in and I never completed my formal theological education. All I could do was trust that God would help me to educate myself. I put legs to my prayers. I saved my money and bought every theological textbook I could afford. And I devoured them. With God's help, I became self-educated. I jokingly tell people that I attended Mary's College – that is, at the feet of Jesus! And let me tell you something: For many years I felt less than complete because I did not have the same seminary degrees as other clergy and religious leaders in my field.

But I'll tell you something else: God has a sense of humor. When we are faithful to God, God has a wonderful way of meeting our deepest needs, healing our hearts, and fulfilling our deepest desires. So it was that in May of 2002, Chicago Theological Seminary, one of the world's preeminent theological schools, appointed me to its Board of Trustees in Chicago, Illinois.

CTS was founded in 1855 and has a rich history of commitment to many spiritual and justice issues that are vital to Metropolitan Community Churches, and to our predominantly gay, lesbian, bisexual and transgender constituency. The school has a strong commitment to cultural and racial diversity, gender justice, and inclusivity of sexual minorities.

CTS faculty and students were activists in the abolitionist movement and the underground railroad prior to the Civil War - and CTS was the first institution of higher learning to give an honorary degree to Martin Luther King, Jr. The school has enjoyed a long and proud association with both the Civil Rights movement and the struggle of South African Christians against apartheid.

Chicago Theological Seminary has been open and welcoming to GLBT students, and many MCC clergy have received their theological training at CTS.

CTS is home to the first distinct Department of Christian Sociology in an American theological school and maintains a close working relationship with both the University of Chicago School of Social Service Administration and the Urban Clinical Pastoral Education (CPE) program.

In 1902, CTS graduated Florence Fensham, the first woman in the United States to prepare for ordination with a Bachelor of Divinity degree.

Today, CTS maintains a two-fold commitment to both

feminist and womanist theological concerns as well as a global engagement to nurture contemporary mature masculine spirituality.

And thus God's sense of humor. It was in Chicago, in 1960, that Christian leaders told me a gay man didn't deserve a Christian education. Now, 42 years later in that same city where I was expelled from Bible college, I now sit as one of the Trustees of this wonderful Seminary that is training Christian leaders from around the world.

Here's another way God has been at work in and through my life:

In 1965, I was drafted into the U. S. military. As all draftees did, I served my required two years of military service. I achieved a top secret NATO crypto clearance and would have died for my country had that been required. I served with distinction in the U. S. Army. Over the years I've been so saddened by the actions of the U.S. government in the treatment of the gay and lesbian communities during wartime and peacetime. In wartime the government will never ask you what you do in your bedroom, they need bodies for the military. But in peacetime our government has always had a policy of denying the right to serve in the military to members of our GLBT community.

It has only been in the last 10 years that the U. S. government put into effect the "Don't Ask, Don't Tell" policy – a policy that was intended to protect our community but which in actuality has had a horrendous and negative impact. In fact, the number of lesbian and gay men discharged based on homosexuality has increased under this policy.

As a human rights activist, I have testified before the U.S. Congress and spoken one-on-one with a President of the United States about this issue. I have spoken on behalf of those in the GLBT communities who wish to honorably serve their country as members of the military services.

As I am fond of saying, God may be slow but God is always on time. In July of 2002, we experienced a major breakthrough that will help us begin to break down barriers with the U.S. government over this issue.

In late July 2002, Metropolitan Community Churches received recognition from the federal government to supply chaplains to the U. S. Veterans Administration. This marks a historic step for our predominantly gay churches. U. S. government programs have long been hostile to GLBT military service members and veterans, so this marks yet another positive step towards full equality for our community.

While independent from the military services, the Veterans Administration provides support and outreach programs to both active duty service members and veterans. The Veterans Administration is the second largest of the 14 cabinet departments in the U.S. Executive Branch and operates world-wide programs for military veterans including health care, financial assistance, vocational rehabilitation, education, training and employment services, as well as management of all military cemeteries. Among its many services , the VA provides health care assistance to more than 100,000 homeless veterans each year. More than 70 million Americans are eligible for VA benefits because they are veterans, family members, or surviving spouses of veterans. The loud, crashing noise I'm hearing right now is the sound of yet another door of oppression being broken open.

Now, what caused this new opportunity for Metropolitan Community Churches to reach out and serve military veterans? Yes, we prayed long and hard for this day. But we also put legs to our prayers. We contacted officials. We filled out applications and government forms. We supplied reams of documentation. We invested staff time and resources.

We combined supernatural prayer with human action - and the result is yet another in a long series of miracles for our GLBT communities.

Listen, my friend, whatever you do in life, don't give up. Keep praying, keep putting those legs on your prayers. When you combine supernatural prayer with human action, miracles will take place in your life.

Let me add another very personal thought: With all the wonderful and amazing things that have occurred in my life, our struggle for social and spiritual justice for GLBT persons is still far from over. There are many prayers I'm still praying. And as long as God gives me breath, I'll do my best to stand up and to speak up for our people who still experience rejection, pain, oppression and hostility.

Troy Perry has devoted his life to help others discover the loving and caring God to whom he has committed his life. As the founder of Metropolitan Community Churches (MCC), he has watched the membership grow from 12 to over 46,000 in the past 35 years.

MCC was the first church to recognize the necessity of ministering to the needs of gays, lesbians, bisexuals and transgendered persons throughout the world. It is through that ministry that Perry has become a leading activist for gay and lesbian rights.

Rev. Perry began his vocation in Florida at the age of 13 and was licensed as a Baptist minister two years later. During this period, he became aware of his sexual orientation and felt – as many gays did in rural America – that he must certainly be the only one in the world who felt that way.

In 1959 he married his pastor's daughter, and a year later Rev. Perry, his wife and newborn son moved to Illinois where Rev. Perry planned to attend Midwest Bible College. While studying at Midwest, Rev. Perry worked for a plastics company that asked him to move to Southern California to open a new plant. Rev. Perry, with his wife and two sons, made the move in 1962.

Once in California Rev. Perry was assigned to pastor the Church of God of Prophecy in Santa Ana. It was there that Rev. Perry experienced an "uneasy" coming out and came to terms with his gayness. He and his wife separated after five years of marriage and later were divorced.

When Rev. Perry returned to Los Angeles after a two-year stint in the army, he was set on the historical course his life was to take.

"The Lord was dealing with me. My previous church taught that you couldn't be a Christian and a gay person, too. I kept this up until one day God got a word in edge-wise and said, 'Don't tell me what I can do. I love you, Troy, and I don't have any stepsons or stepdaughters. Reread my Word.' And reread God's word I did."

It was following a close friend's arrest that Rev. Perry realized that "God cares," precipitating the birth of MCC in Los Angeles, and ultimately leading to the birth of Metropolitan Community Churches, which has grown to 300 congregations in 23 countries.

Rev. Perry's activism has taken many turns during the past 35 years, including positions on a number of boards of gay, lesbian, bisexual and transgendered organizations. He held a seat on the Los Angeles County Commission on Human Relations. In 1978 he was honored by the American Civil Liberties Union Lesbian and Gay Rights Chapter with its Humanitarian Award. He holds honorary doctorates from Episcopal Divinity School (Boston), Samaritan College (Los Angeles), and Sierra University (Santa Monica), California for his work in civil rights, and was recently lauded by the Gay Press Association with its Humanitarian Award. Rev. Perry was invited to the White House in 1977 by President Jimmy Carter to discuss the gay and lesbian civil rights, and was a guest of President Bill Clinton at the 1997 White House Conference on Hate Crimes.

In addition to his work as a gay religious leader and human rights activist, Rev. Perry has found time to write an autobiography, "The Lord is My Shepherd and Knows I'm Gay." Rev. Perry also completed a sequel to this book, titled "Don't Be Afraid Anymore," published by St. Martin's Press. He is a contributing editor for the book "Is Gay Good?" and the subject of another book, "Our God Too."

For Information On Ordering Additional Copies:

Write to:

Metropolitan Community Churches

8704 Santa Monica Boulevard, 2nd Floor

West Hollywood, CA 90069

E-Mail:

info@MCCchurch.org

For A Free Subscription To The MCC Newsletter,

Send Your E-Mail Address To:

info@MCCchurch.org

For The Latest Information

On Metropolitan Community Churches, Visit

www.MCCchurch.org